PICASSO

HIS RECENT DRAWINGS

1966 – 1968

PICASSO

HIS RECENT DRAWINGS

1966 – 1968

PREFACE BY RENÉ CHAR

TEXT BY CHARLES FELD

Harry N. Abrams, Inc. *Publishers* New York

Milton S. Fox, *Editor-in-Chief*

Translated by Suzanne Brunner

Standard Book Number: 8109-0381-4

Library of Congress Catalogue Card Number: 77-90893

Harry N. Abrams, Incorporated, New York

Copyright 1969 in France by Éditions Cercle d'Art, Paris

Illustrations printed in France. Text printed in the Netherlands

Bound in the Netherlands

CONTENTS

A Thousand Planks for a Life-Raft 7

Picasso Today 13

The Plates 25

List of Plates 249

A Thousand Planks for a Life-Raft

1939

Thanks to Picasso in that most severely tried province of painting, that of the foliation of objects through the rigorous adjustment of faces and shapes set against one another, Light and its servant, the Hand, will have fulfilled their temporal destiny: they will have overflowed the economy of creation, expanded man's gestures, incited him to greater demands, knowledge, and inventiveness. This is taking place, universally. But... terror surrounds us and Nazism, that artistic antilife, is gradually seizing every lever of activity and leisure; it is making ready to rule as absolute slaughterer. Consciously or unintentionally provident, Picasso's work has known how to raise for the spirit, long before this terror existed, a counter-terror which we must take hold of and use to best avail in the infernal situations soon to engulf us. Against totalitarian power, Picasso is master craftsman of a thousand planks for a life-raft.

Without appearing declinable, his contribution would seem to proceed by lunar cycles. He who pierces through immunity, chiromancer of the death thrust, the artist must be seen as full of fear, he slashes away at the excess of reality of his model with his draftsman's or his colorist's sword, then to indemnify us with the offering of their essence. Everywhere, from the mischievous Minotaur to the young women of Mougins, from the heads riddled with words of escape to the sublime drabness of Guernica, there rings out the call: "Stand up and fight, you Wolves, the battle is on!" Vermillion flares up, scarlet yields to it, but at a distance from the picture.

July 1939, in the hypnotic trance of Paris, capital foresworn, let us break away, without weakening, from that which sum-

mons us, and resume awhile life together with our Melusinas and the utensils of our youth.... Dear Picasso, Don Giovanni!

1969

Thirty years! Picasso has since then left several planets, having equipped and warmed them to the brim. It is Desire against Power, desire which always prevails and will prevail in this admirable killer; he bears in him wrath and love conjoined, non-function and function. And nothing is more unsure than that which we hold as certainty against him.

Call God? Nothing. Recall the gods: they will come. The libertines have not fallen asleep.

Picasso Today

Since the beginning of the century, Picasso has lavished upon us an œuvre of youthful abundance. He has marked the memory of entire generations with an image of the world fashioned by the distinctive quality of his art. That this art has made so deep an impression proves that Picasso's creative process has been free of all restraint and constantly oriented toward the future. In perpetual motion, his work is the visual transcript of the profound aspirations of millions of men and women. Together with the best of these, the artist refuses to submit to the rules and restrictions of the past, and he has endeavored to eradicate those traditions that are rooted in falsehood.

Picasso holds a privileged place at the artistic center of our time because his œuvre—so diversified both in substance and in form—mirrors the vital problems of humanity. He has become a beacon that guides us along the uncertain paths of contemporary life, the strong shaft of light that illuminates the darkest corners, the prism that reflects the myriad aspects of reality.

The fact that he constantly reappraises his own achievements and follows uncharted roads may have dampened the enthusiasm of his early admirers. Still, his progress along new paths and away from conformity has earned him the faithful allegiance of innumerable traveling companions. While he has had to bear the terrible solitude that is the lot of all creative

artists, it has not kept him from spreading his "giant wings." His œuvre can be read like an intimate journal on a universal scale, in which the biographical elements are clearly discernible even as they give way to the torrent of contemporary life; tumultuous waves engulf his art and bring forth from their depths Man as he appears in our time. Often troubled and beset by anxiety, Picasso continues on his solitary way. And he is often torn between his own desire, the impulse of a generous nature toward friendship with his peers, and the responsibility of being true to himself alone.

DEFYING ONE'S OWN CERTAINTIES

This contradictory, zigzagging transmutation of solitude into solicitude toward his fellow man is the exact measure of Picasso's independence and artistic freedom; rejecting both system and routine, it makes of his art a prodigious adventure. He is able to maintain a kind of aloofness toward his own artistic creation and toward the subject on which it is loosely and freely based. Yet he never loses sight of nature, of the universe that surrounds us. By re-creating it in his personal imagery he makes it his own. Picasso is a debunker of reality who draws on nature for the elements of his choice. These he translates onto paper by way of a subtle interaction of thought and hand. The result is a language made of signs and images, vibrant with life. He gathers the whole world into himself and projects it in his work. In this respect we find not one but several Picassos. There is not just one "evolution" of his art, a logical progression proceeding in successive stages, but rather a permanent state of metamorphosis, a spontaneous and perpetual outpouring of creativity that is a basic unity unto itself. Whichever medium he decides to use—brush, pen, burin, or pencil—he finds himself each time before a new challenge that he must meet. Each new creation is a test to which he must submit, an obstacle to be conquered. These tasks he sets himself are the points of reference that mark his entire working life, and he

appears to us much like a tireless pioneer carving an arduous jungle path through a dense and hostile vegetation.

THE TRUTH OF OUR TIME

If we are to believe Ingres, according to whom "drawing is the candid image of art," then Picasso has never expressed his own truth more completely than during this highly prolific period of his life: two years during which he produced thousands of drawings.

Drawings are of major importance in his œuvre, and it would be absurd to try to assign a hierarchy of values to one type or another. Just as it would be pointless to value a drawing according to the period during which it was done. For Picasso, what matters is the truth of his time as he sees it. Truth, the purpose and the creative impulse of his art. So many of his superb drawings enrich museums and private collections throughout the world. Yet it was never Picasso's intention to provide an academic lesson on the meaning of beauty. He often says that beauty is an abstract notion, as volatile and fleeting as time itself. Beauty is never anything but the idea we conceive of it at a given moment. It is impossible, therefore, to hold a fixed opinion about it, to canonize what we consider to be eternally beautiful in the manner in which traditional art for so many centuries congealed its ideas of what beauty should be. Picasso has said that "an artist paints so as to free himself of his impressions and of his visions." It is a constant hand-to-hand combat between him and the subject from which he tries to wrest that fundamental grain of truth—regardless of whether this truth bears a joyous or a frightening countenance. Attached as it is to life in its most intimate aspects, his art probes life's secrets while showing us its intricate course. That is why Picasso cannot let himself be imprisoned behind the bars of formalistic themes, however rich they may be. His incurably inquiring mind, his capacity for new impressions, for ever renewed sensations, infuse his work with intensity and a deep, rich vitality. Some of his critics accuse him of inconsistency; instead he should be praised for being constant to his own guiding principles. It is an uninterrupted battle between the emotions and their sacrifice on the altar of artistic freedom.

For this reason also Picasso cannot be satisfied with only one form of expression. He did not limit himself to drawings during the two years which concern us here; he also painted, and made pottery, cartoons for tapestries, and engravings. He did, however, produce literally thousands of drawings, and these represent the essence of his activity during this time. That is why we attach such great importance to these 405 drawings we have chosen to reproduce in this volume.

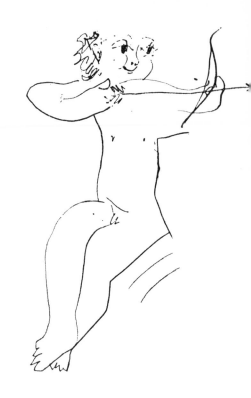

TO SEE IS TO UNDERSTAND

The greatness of these drawings lies in their realism, which shows a totality rather than fragmentary aspects. Whether the persons depicted by Picasso are clad in antique garb, or dressed as musketeers, or appear as nature created them, they are not timeless—they are the men and women of today. They do not turn us away from reality. On the contrary, they constantly return us to reality. To a reality which is the product of a guiding thought, of emotions, of a sense of responsibility that brings us an unadorned vision of a universe where each of us has a well-determined place.

Ignore the disguises that cloak Picasso's people. Ignore the imaginary situations to which they are subjected.

In these drawings, published here for the first time, all styles cross, collide, or harmonize. The mythological cupid meets the pastoral flute player; the watermelon eater fraternizes with the booted musketeer; the painter in his collaret brings forth from his palette thousands of nudes; the sad-faced horse carries a dainty circus rider on its back; the face of a man, features deeply etched by experience, gives way to a mask showing eye sockets empty of eyes; women whose shapely bodies invite the games of love offer or refuse themselves to gent-

lemen rejoicing in their virility or saddened at having to admit to their weakness. The most intimate scenes alternate with the public spectacle of the circus. A whole universe emerges with man at its center and master of all creation. Man, his head wreathed with flowers as fragile and as tenacious as hope.

Picasso does not depict specific historical situations, nor are his characters inanimate puppets; they are as alive as though made of flesh and blood. Through them a dialogue emerges, suspended as it were in time and space, but more intense and more real than reality.

Picasso goes beyond appearances. He tears away the veils of illusion and contrivance that obscure our vision of life, which presents itself to us as fragmentary, fixed, and almost abstract. He obliges us to look at the world around us and to see beyond its various and scattered elements—pictorial, emotional, or symbolic. He breaks down the barriers that separate us from a reality that is ours to influence and to transform rather than to contemplate passively as though it were a spectacle that does not concern us. Picasso's acuity of vision sharpens our own intelligence. Its effect is like fresh water that washes away all preconceived ideas, all irrelevancies. Our senses reawakened, he restores to us a kind of lucidity that is akin to innocence. Thanks to him, we look with new eyes upon a world where it feels good to breathe, to be alive, to taste fresh spring water or a loaf of bread still warm from the oven. Having thus returned to a state of simplicity, we find ourselves once again able to savor all that life has to offer.

A CONSTANT RENEWAL

The new cycle of Picasso's œuvre that starts with this volume dates from March 27, 1966 to March 15, 1968. All the themes found in Picasso's earlier work reappear here, like well-known personalities whose familiar features we recognize. We had left them at some point in their lives and now rediscover them a little later, more mature, and pick up the thread of a story inter-

rupted for a while. These characters may seem unchanged, but their significance is totally different. Much water has flowed under the bridge since we first made their acquaintance. A return to the past is not a systematic device in Picasso's œuvre, and he does not use it on a purely intellectual level. Life, like a river depositing a fertile alluvial soil, has enriched the experience of Picasso's cast of characters. In depicting them as he sees them the artist also reveals the humor, the irony, and the wisdom he has gained over the years, and thus, the new and at the same time more positive and more subtle relationship that binds him to the world.

Picasso is too deeply preoccupied with the present to revive the past or to dwell in nostalgia. On the contrary. The classical themes he uses in some of his drawings prove once again the distance that separates him from them, from the ordinary worldly taboos, from the kind of art which needs deconsecrating and which he ridicules with such satisfaction and high good humor.

LET US ENJOY HONEST SENSUALITY

Why should we be shocked or pretend to be shocked by the frankly and openly erotic character of these exquisite drawings? They are alive with an all-consuming *joie de vivre*. They evoke for us the heat of a sandy beach warmed by the Mediterranean sun, the cool ocean, the lightness of the air, the transparent blue of the sky. Whatever their form or the medium used, they impress us with the tenderness or cruelty they reflect, the irony or the bitter sorrow. In any case, there is nothing questionable or vulgar about them. These drawings are of a quality that is as rich and as complex as human nature. One can almost feel the heartbeat of these lovers living in a universe in which reality produces its own dream of peace, of happiness and serenity.

I know of nothing more chaste than these female or male nudes, even though, for reasons unknown, the female nude is more generally accepted than the male. We shall leave the

elucidation of this mystery to the more ponderous among us. Ever since the Immaculate Conception we have known for a fact that prudes cannot tolerate the idea of caresses or carnal desire. They are pure in spirit and of gloomy disposition. As for the rest of us, let us not hesitate to steep ourselves joyously in this atmosphere of honest sensuality. We have no need for the restraints of a moral philosophy devoid of true morality.

Humanity would have disappeared long ago had our ancestors actually followed the edifying and virtuous edicts of hypocrites whose way of life is based on the formula: "Do as I say, not as I do."

Anatomy does not change because this or that part of the human body is removed from sight. The artist, in any case, has the right to bring his subjects to life in all their reality. Picasso does so freely and without preconceived ideas.

One does not honor the dignity of man by rigging him out in a fig leaf, and the noblest passions are degraded when scaled down to the dimensions of a breechcloth. As when, in the past, Truth was shown allegorically emerging naked from a well, but without the attributes of its nakedness. Such an omission was in itself a travesty of Truth.

REALMS OF FANCY BORN OF REALITY

During these two years of intensive work, Picasso was not simply carried away by an impulsive and pleasurable desire to glorify the human form. In a world in the process of complete transformation and upheaval, at a time when man is preparing to conquer nature on an ever grander scale, a new "universe of form and of design" is in the process of creation. It manifests itself as an irrepressible need.

Where do we come from? Where are we going? The age-old questions concerning the destiny of man—his place in society, the part he is to play as a passenger on the planet earth, the need to know more about himself—become obsessive, and the quest for answers ever more urgent. Picasso looks at hu-

manity and observes its struggle. And, out of a deep inner necessity, he re-creates what he sees in his œuvre.

Man is not deified by the artist, nor placed above his station. Picasso's attitude is that of a critic. The specific value of his work lies not in those elements which he derives from the artistic heritage of the past, but in the personal vision of an artist who gives us his own interpretation of the world and its contents. He answers the questions by using observation and thought. He gives them a new and deeper meaning. He creates his own visual reality out of his thoughts and feelings. His art expresses the experiences and impressions that have touched and influenced his life. Thus, comic and tragic aspects of the world exist in his œuvre side by side, heightened by the sureness and lightness of touch that he brings to his drawings.

THE LANGUAGE OF ART

Picasso does not imitate the artists of the past any more than they copied those masters that had preceded them. When Poussin referred to antiquity he did so in order to draw on an existing vocabulary and thereby to create his own language of artistic expression. Artistic truth, in the same way as the artistic image which reflects it, is like a subterranean river that slowly digs its bed, shifting and altering its course as it proceeds. It finds its way to the surface in different places and at different times. It seldom represents the achievement of one man alone, and the expression of the artist when his œuvre is able to mirror reality is merely a brief emergence along the way. The role of the true artist is to enable his fellow man to travel with him for a while on the long journey between ignorance and knowledge.

Art is a demanding master. The problems it raises recur from century to century, like a skein of universal dimensions, with ill-defined contours and intermingled threads. Its messages are whispered and obscurely phrased, and the thoughts it formulates are at times incomplete and at times half-stated like half-remem-

bered dreams. Art is like the combination to a complicated lock for which one number is always missing. For an artist the unending search for greater perfection is the true meaning of art. For humanity has not forgotten anything it has experienced throughout its past. It attaches small value to the present, which is only a brief span of time between yesterday and tomorrow. And so, if certain artistic criteria are replaced by others, who can tell whether they are irrevocably displaced or whether they may not regain favor at some later time and under more auspicious circumstances.

Balzac considered himself the modest secretary who simply made note of the multiple phases of the human condition which he evoked and recorded in book after book. As for Picasso, has he not given us a visual monument filled with poetry and spanning the world? His œuvre includes all that is immediately perceptible—the tangible, obvious meaning, and beyond that the deeper, hidden meaning, as difficult to define as a secret, distant perfume.

Picasso's œuvre includes countless nudes—male and female, misshapen and harmonious, obese and emaciated, giants with abundant forms and dwarfs with strange proportions, bent old men and youths as shapely and full of life as young trees. By contrasting one with the other he shows us the unquenchable beauty of nature in its endless variety. It is to nature and the whole of creation that he devotes his art. We need not be unduly surprised, therefore, if a new world, both imaginary and real, appears in his work year after year. Each time he shows us with infinite variety such themes as the painter and his model, clowns, acrobats and other circus folk, languorous or spirited odalisks moving through the contemporary scene, faces lined with age, shepherds, flute players, bathers. Disguised, their faces masked or freely exposed, these characters posed in theatrical or mythological scenes lead lives of their own against their special backgrounds. They follow their primitive instincts and are intensely alive, bruising themselves on the sharp edges of reality.

There is in Picasso's œuvre a permanence of thought that characterizes all his works and binds them one to the other. The ideas he illustrates return time after time, always modified and newly enriched. With extraordinary obstinacy Picasso pursues his attempt to conquer reality, to which each of his works bears witness. He delves deep into space and penetrates the very essence of people and things. He does so with "both fury and love" as René Char, the poet, has phrased it in his preface to this book.

The story told in Char's preface testifies to Picasso's unity of ideas, to his faithfulness to earlier commitments despite the changing circumstances of his life and the passing years. The beginning of his text was written in 1939, during the turmoil of the outbreak of World War II. It is a miracle that he could rediscover his manuscript so many years later. In 1969 he had the opportunity to pick up where he had left off and to complete it as though nothing had happened during the intervening years. However, as he points out, Picasso had meanwhile "created several worlds and left them behind." Picasso's entire œuvre is the expression of a profound humanism and sense of humanity. And while he brings to his work the infinite resources of his talent, his imagination, and his ideas, the fact remains that he finds his true inspiration in the history of man. The whole world and all of life are the soil and nourishment on which he thrives. And Picasso sees what others cannot. Picasso hears the voices of both live and inanimate things, sounds to which others are deaf. It is this highly flavored fare that sustains his creative energy. Paul Klee has said: "Art does not imitate that which is visible in nature, it *creates* the visible." Picasso moves so quickly that he gets there even before things become visible. He himself has said: "If you wish to draw, close your eyes and sing."

Since our ambition is of necessity more limited, let us open our eyes wide and sing with pleasure as we enjoy the drawings of Picasso

1

3

21.4.66. I
23.7.66.
Picasso

4

5

6

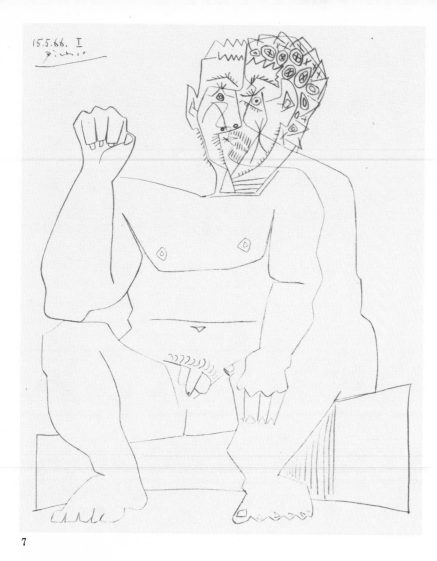

7

8

9

16.5.66. I

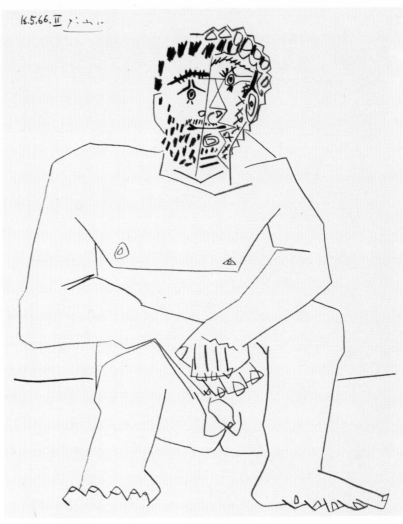

16.5.66. II

11

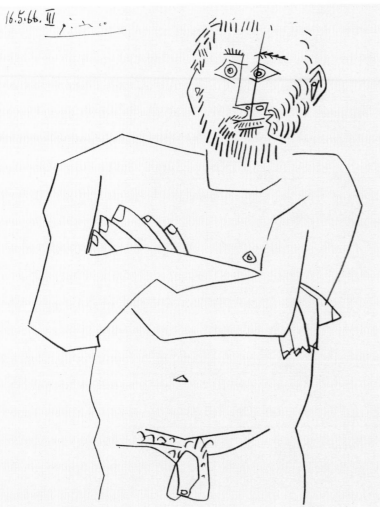

16.5.66. III

16.5.66. IV

13

8.6.66. I

15

16

18

19

20

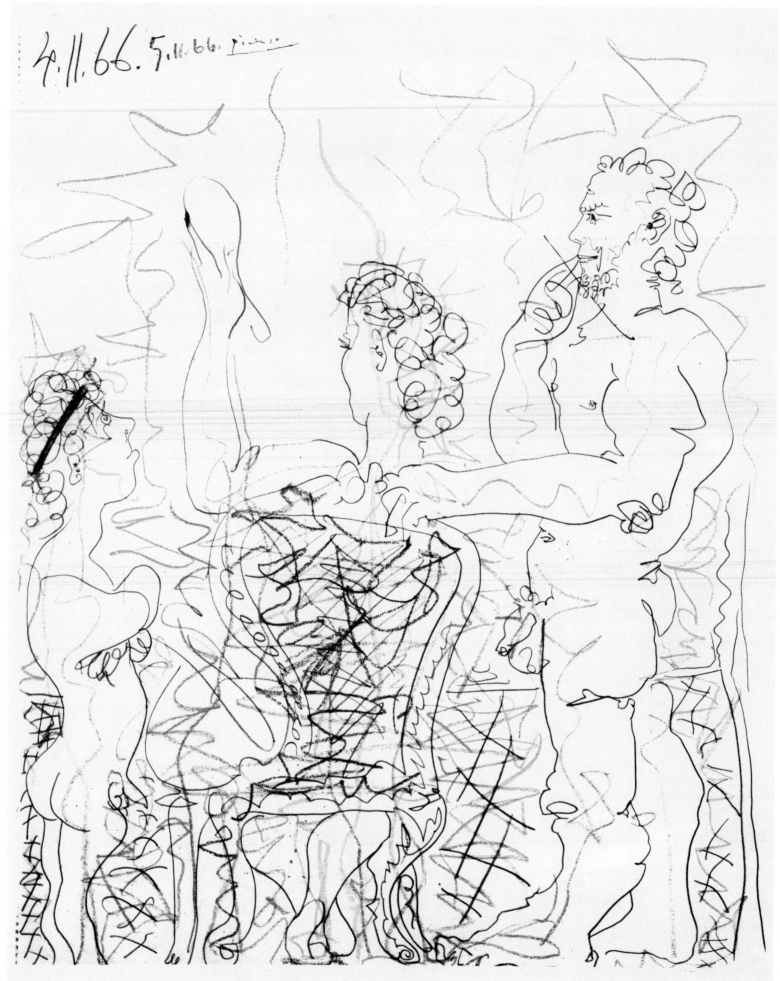

4.11.66. 5.11.66. Picasso

21

30.11.66. I

22

30.11.66. II

23

1er 12.66.

24

27

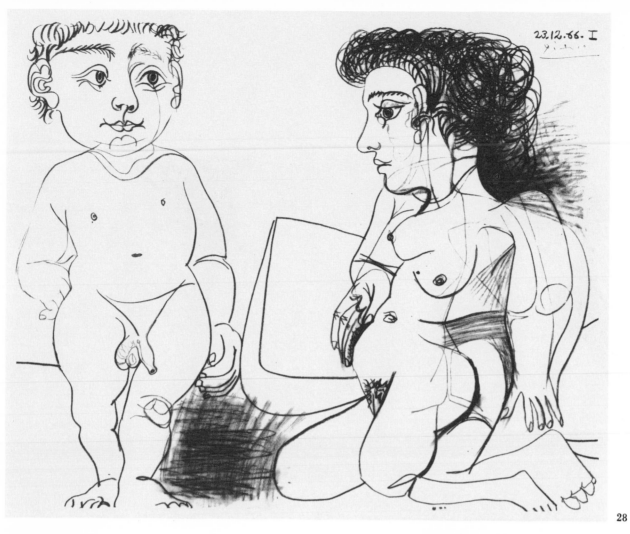

23.12.66. I

28

23.12.66. II

29

30

31

24.12.66.

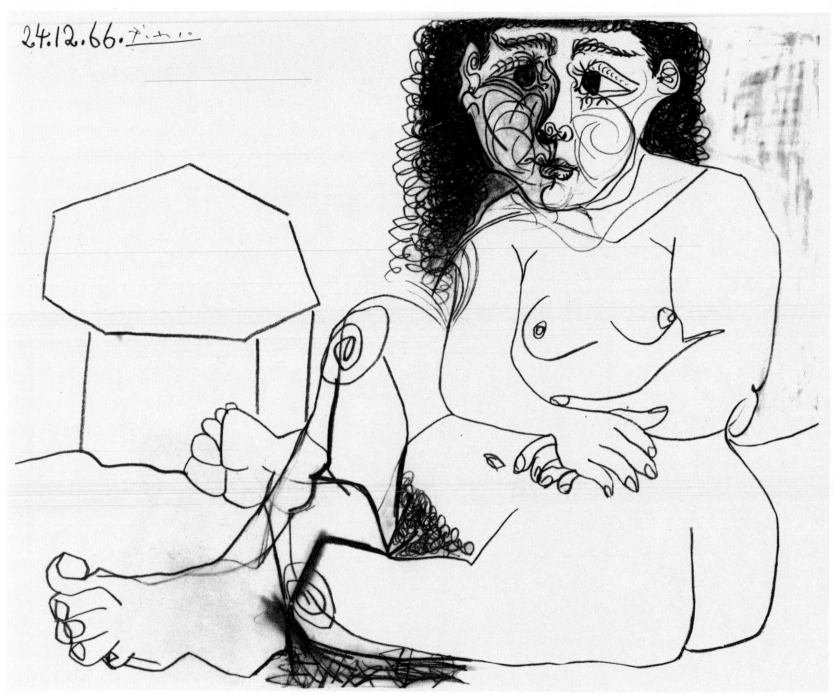

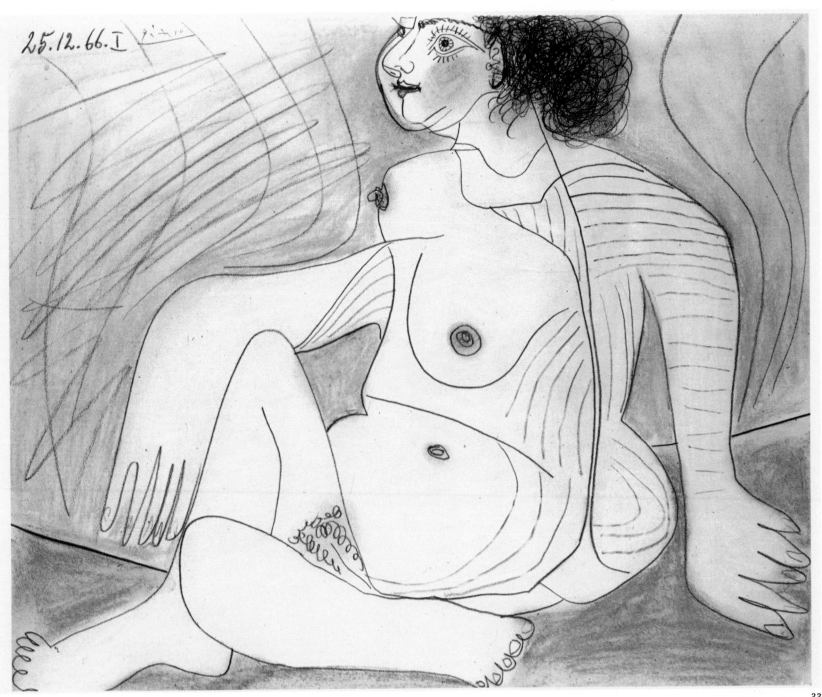

25.12.66. I Picasso

33

34

36

35

26.12.66. I

38

39

42

40

41

43

44

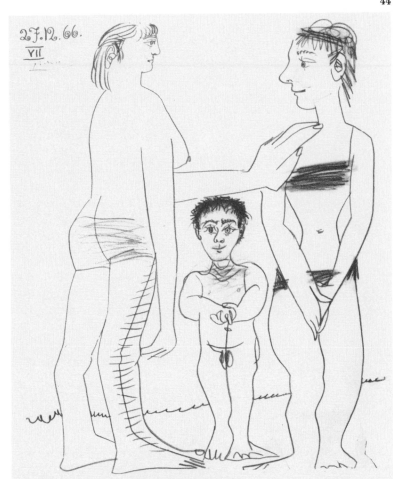

45

46

29.12.66 III

48

49

51

52

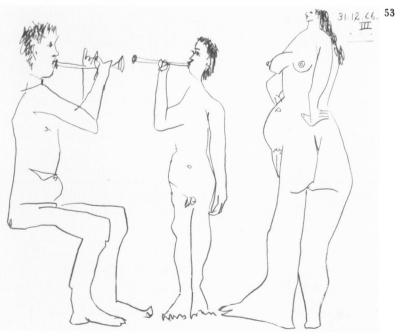

53

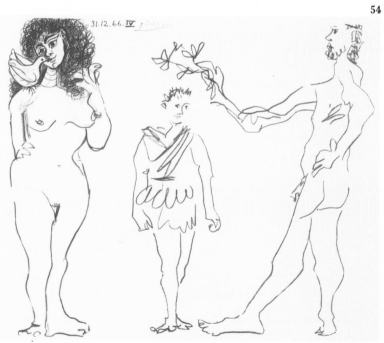

54

55

56

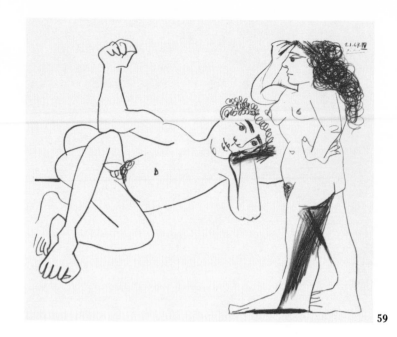

59

57

60

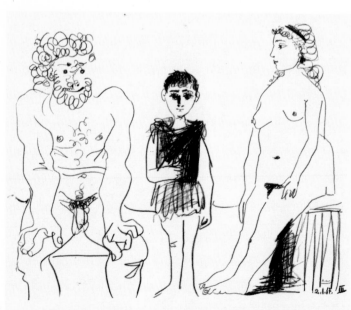

58

61

63

64

62

65

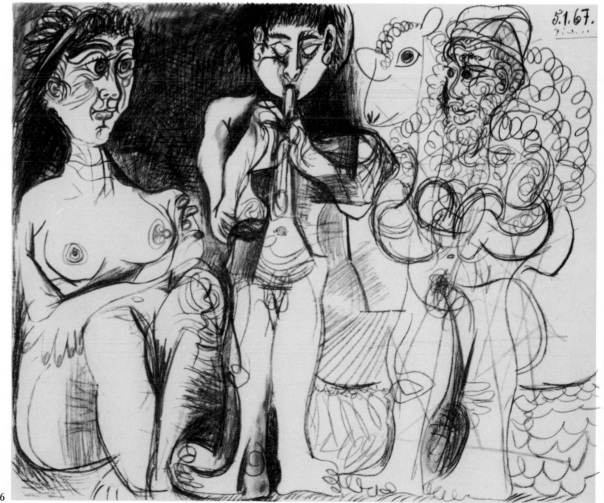

66

67

68

69

70

71

73

74

72

75

79

80

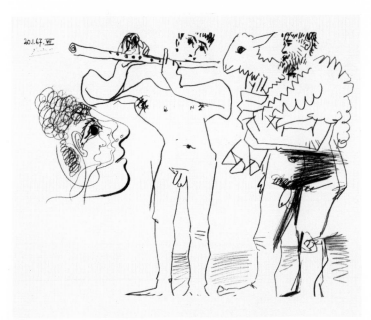

81

82

83

84

85

87

88

89

90

91

92

93

94

96

97

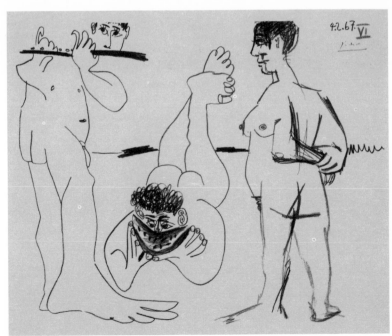

98

99

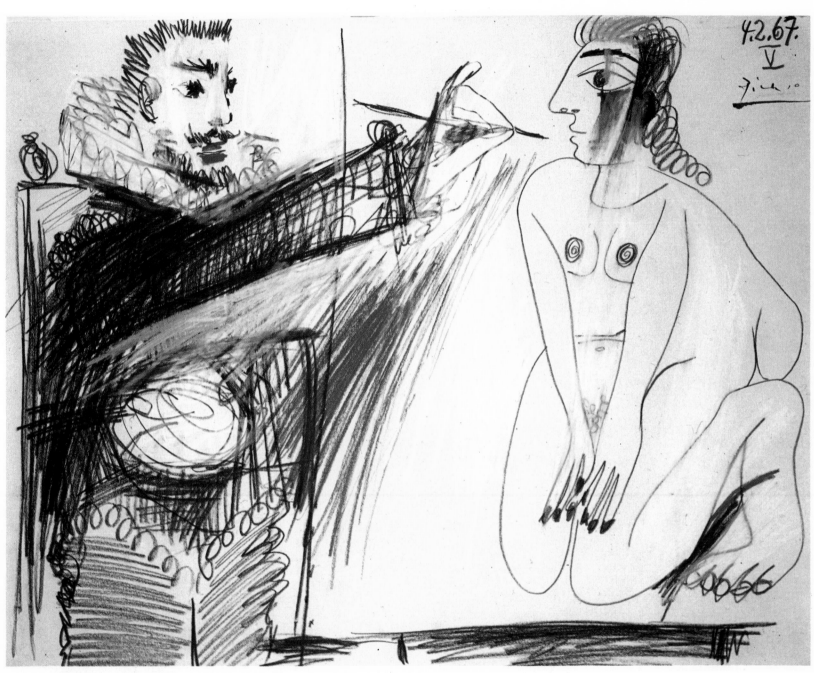

100

101

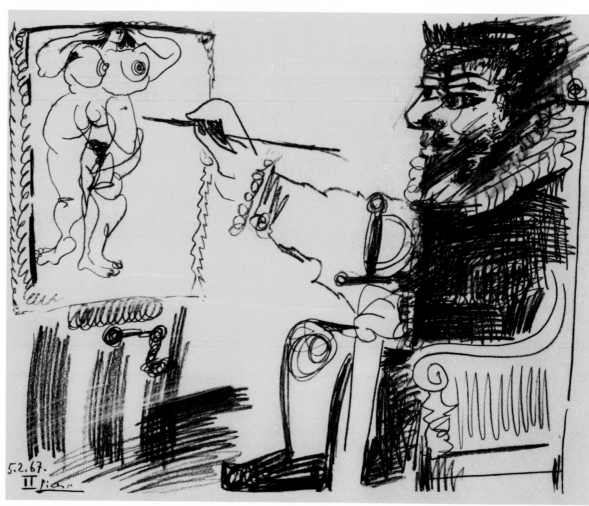

102

103

104

105

106

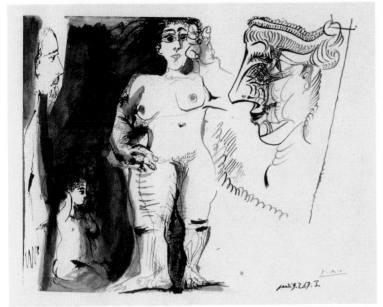

107

108

109

110

111

30.2.67.I
Picasso

112

113

114

115

11.2.67. I Picasso

11.7.67.
III

119

22.2.6

122

123

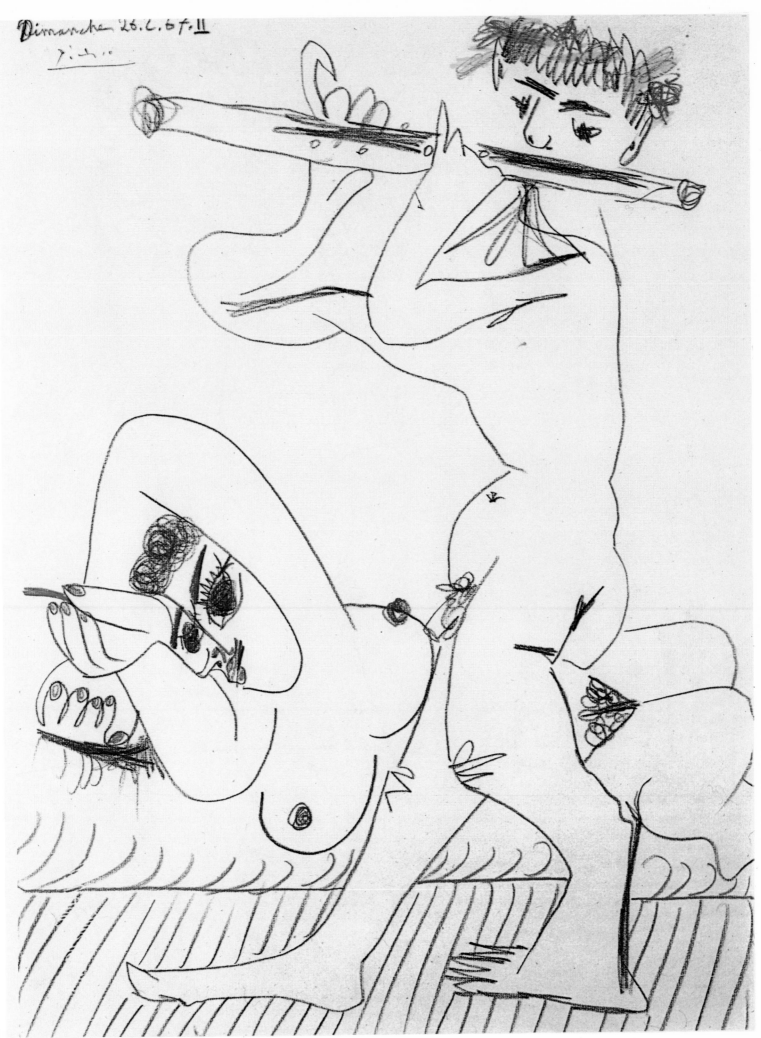

124

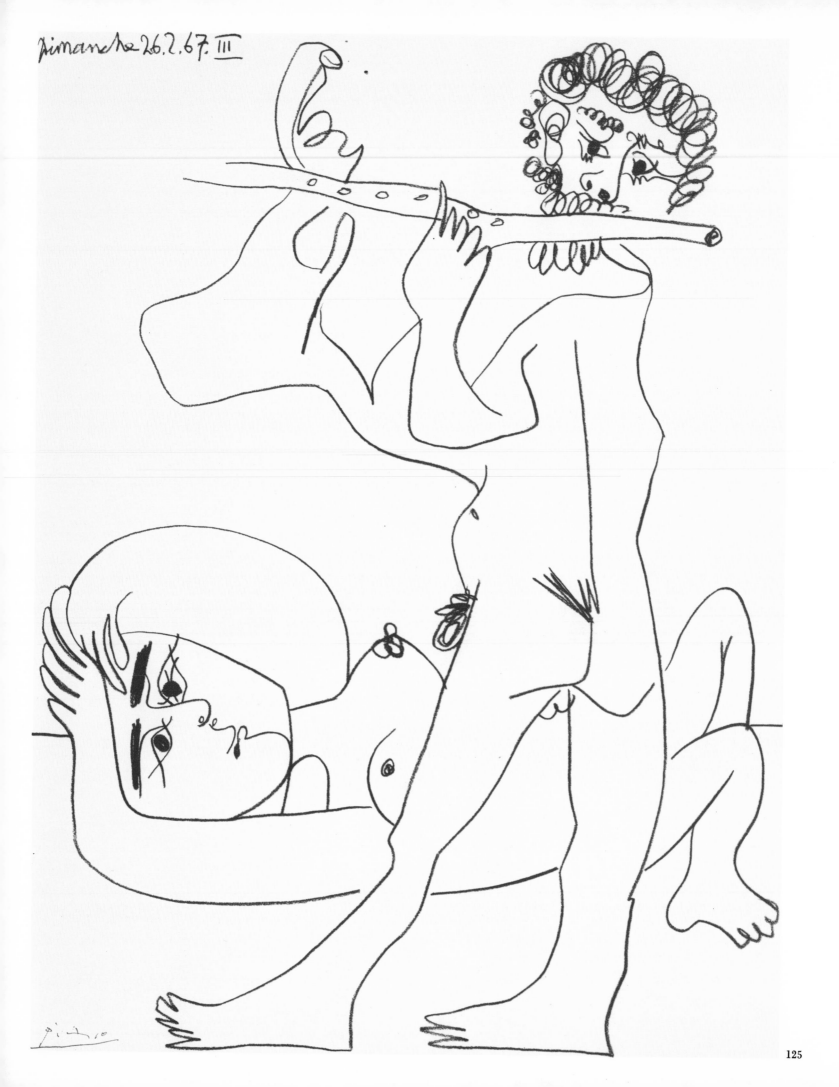

dimanche 26.2.67. III

125

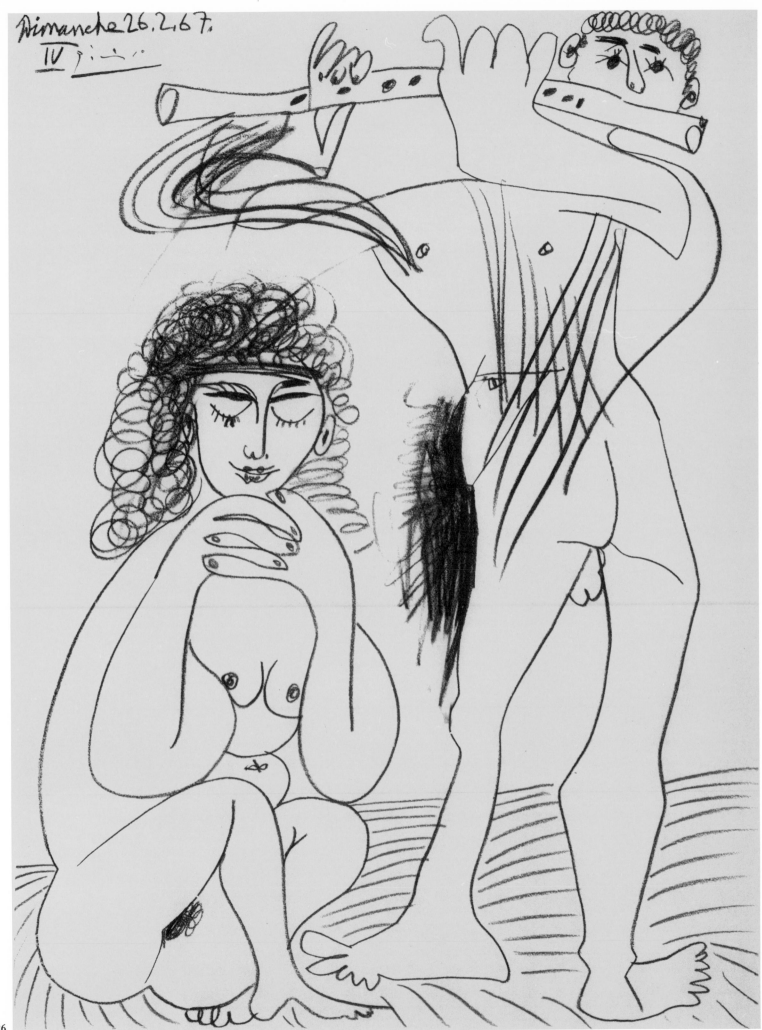

128

130

129

131

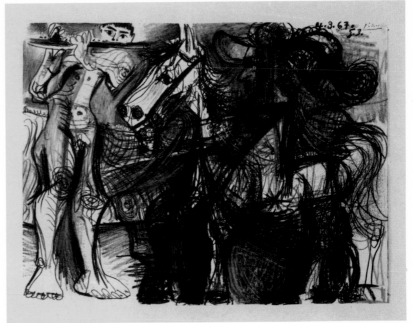

133

134

135

132

136

137

138

139

140

141

142

143

144

146

145

148

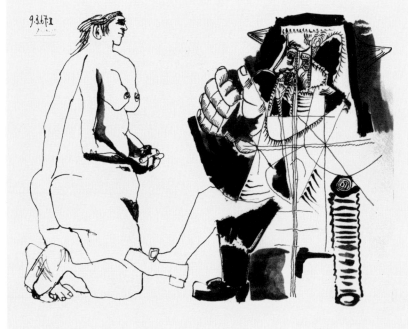

147

149

150

151

152

153

154

155

156

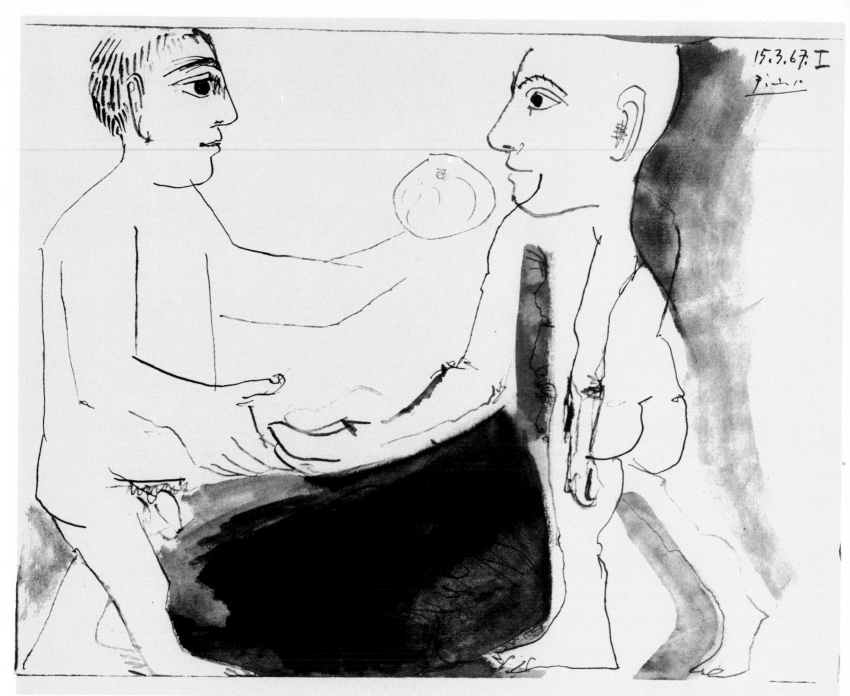

157

15.3.67.II

158

159

15.3.67.
17. IV
18. Picasso

160

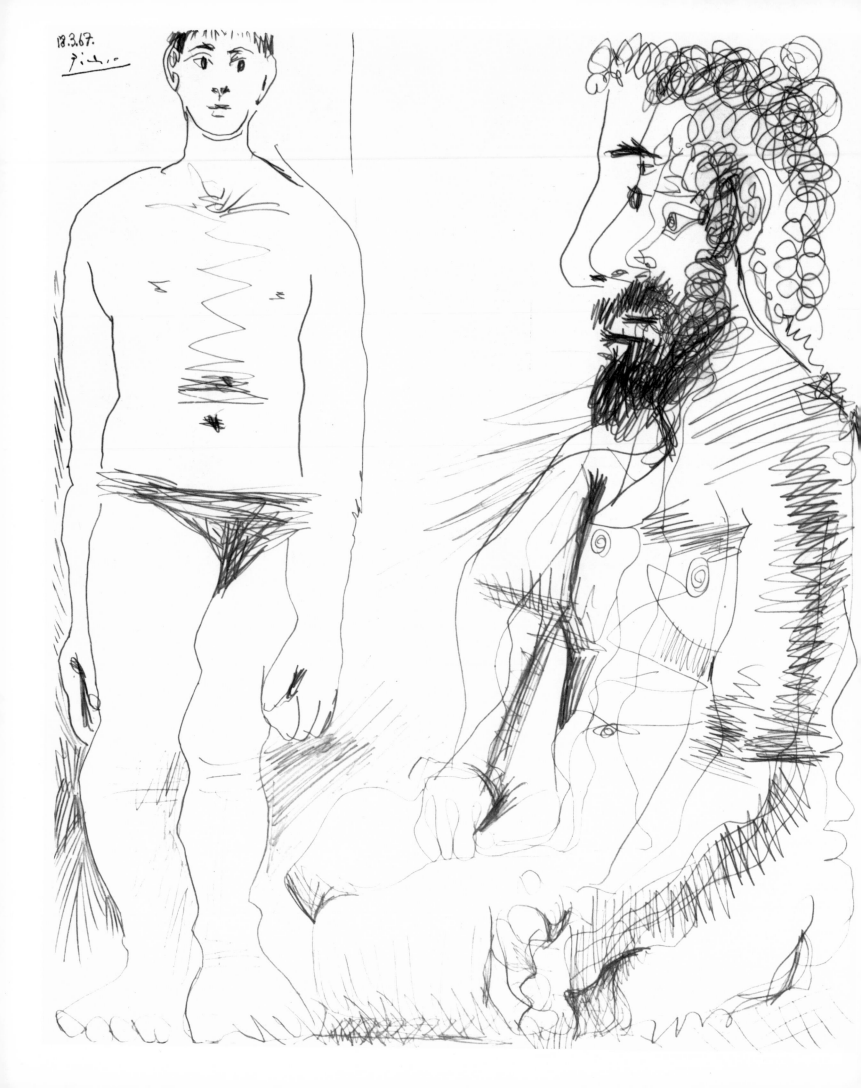

162

163

295.67.

164

165

166

168

170

169

172

173

174

175

177

178

179

182

28.6.67.
II

183

28.6.67.
IV

188

189

190

191

192

1.7.67. IV

194

197

195

198

196

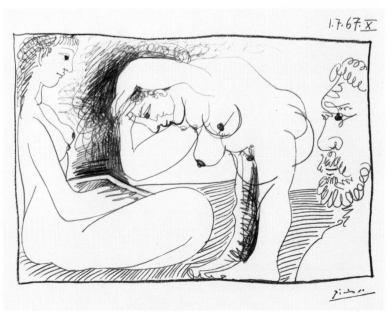

199

202

203

204

205

206

207

208

209

210

211

212

213

214

216

215

217

127.67·I

218

220

219

12.7.67.
II

13.7.67.
Picasso

221

222

223

224

225

226

227

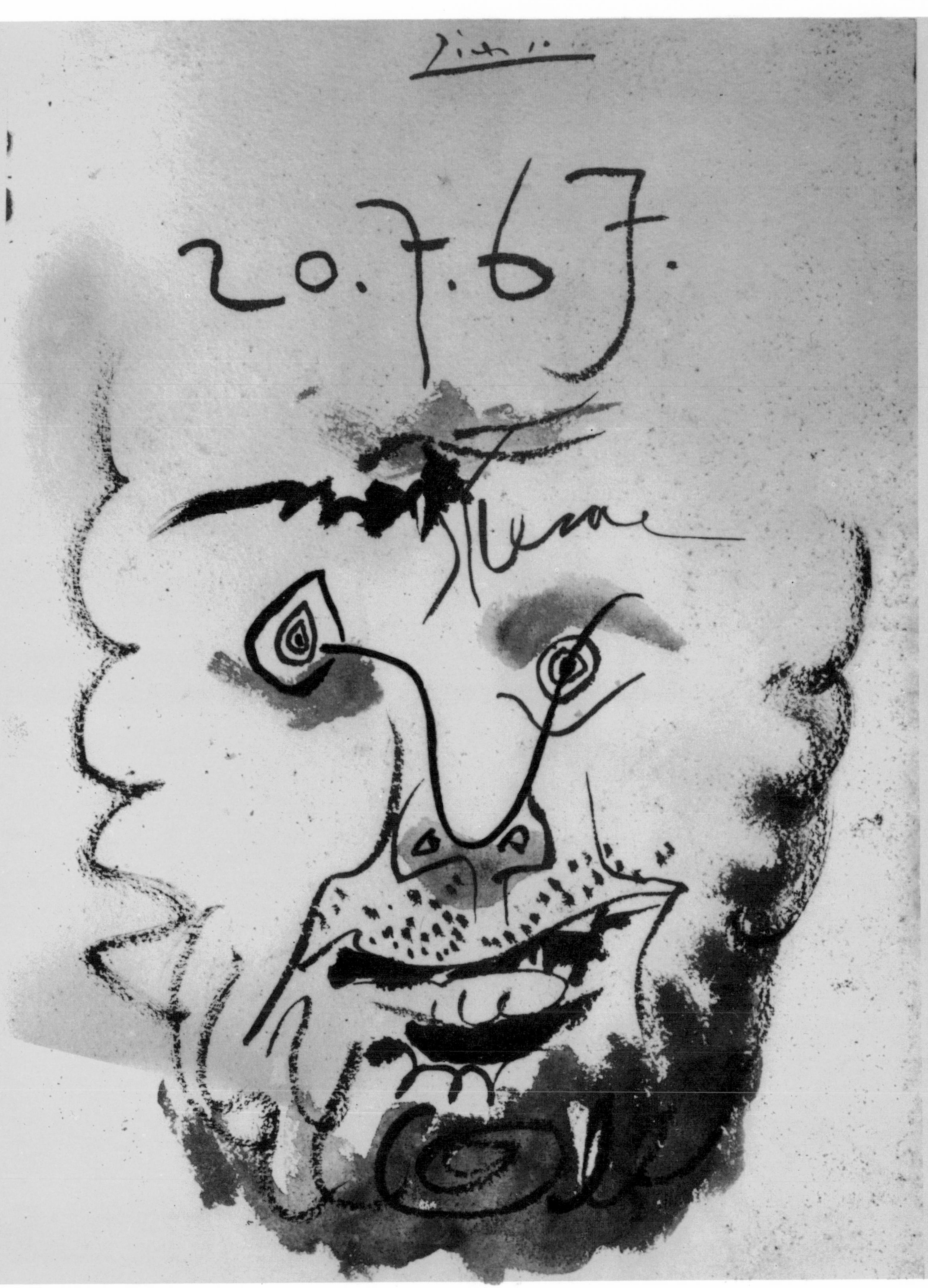
20.7.67.

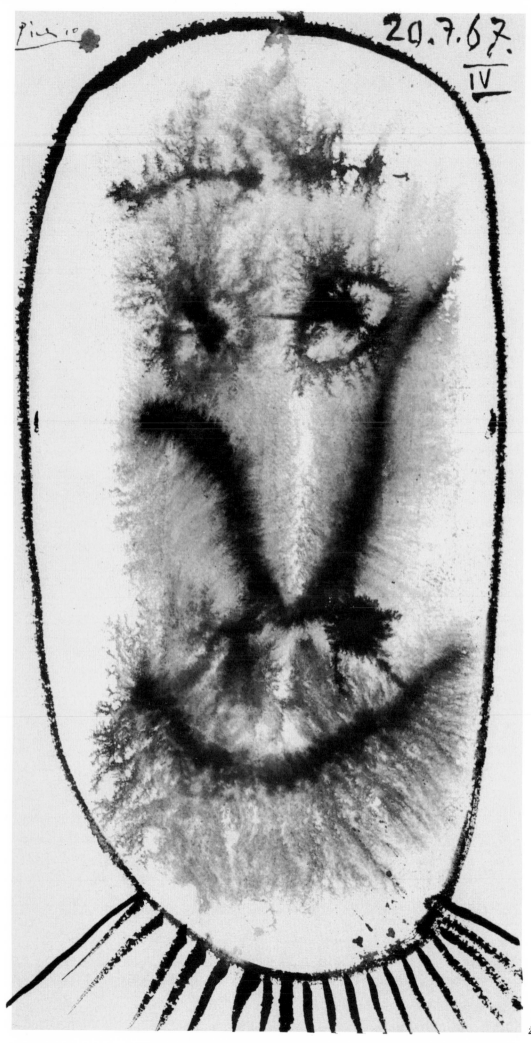

229

230

231

232

233

235

234

236

237

238

239

240

241

242

248

249

252

250

253

251

254

255

257

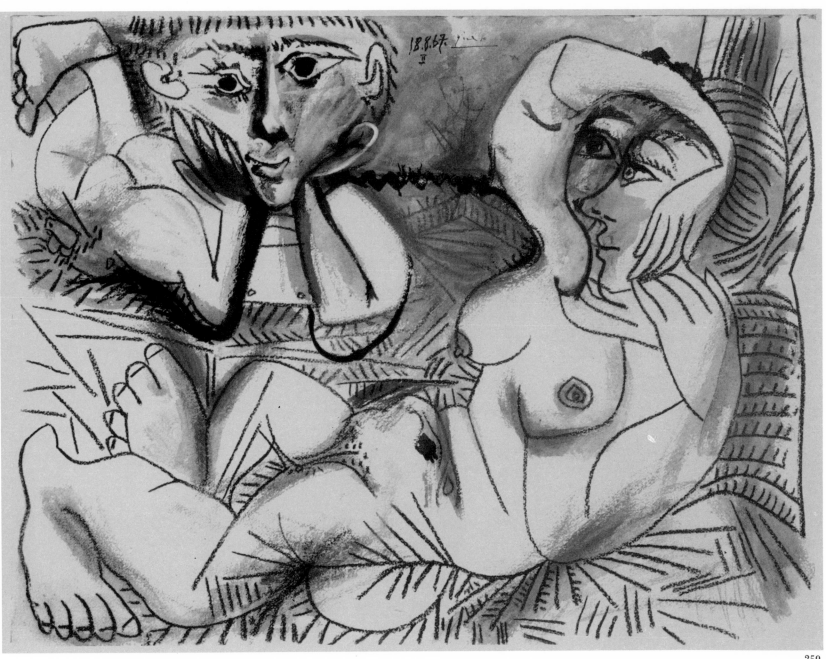

259

260

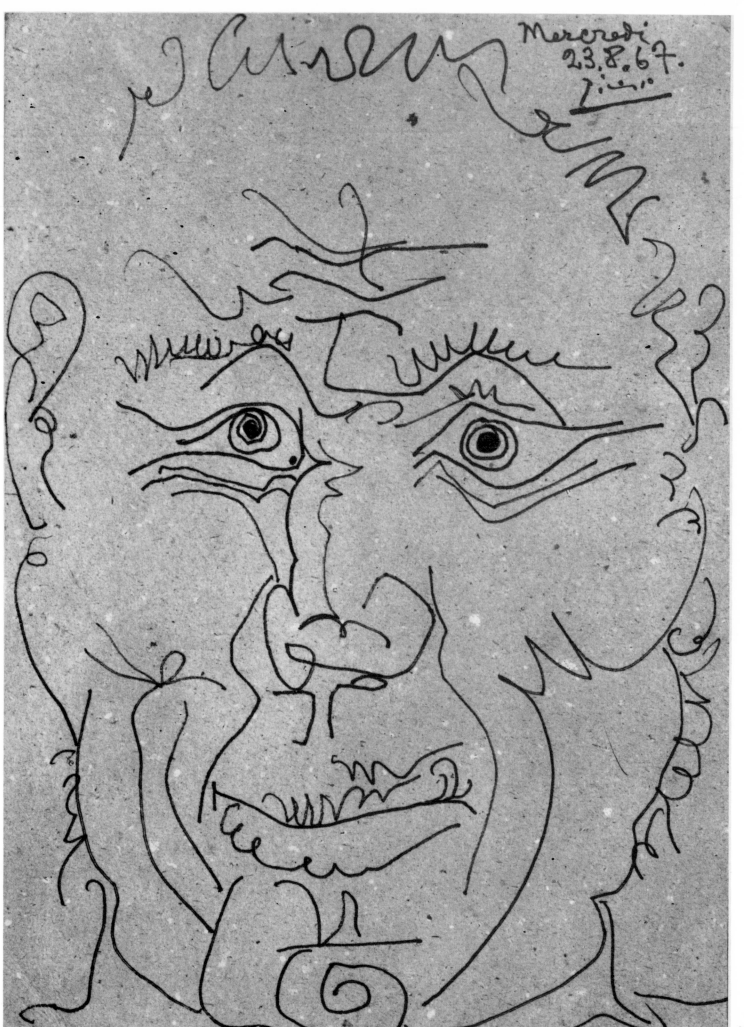

261

263

262

264

265

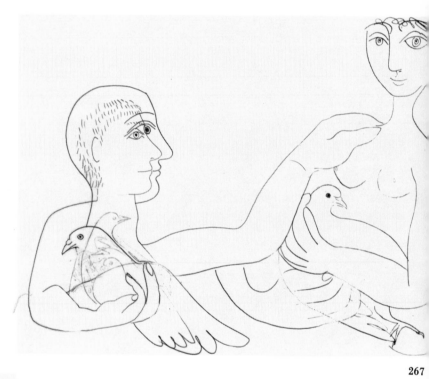

267

266

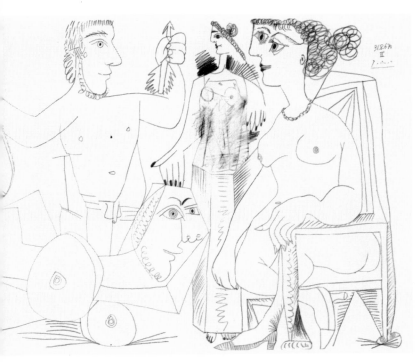

271

272

273

274

275

2.9.67. I
picasso

276

277

3.9.67.I
Picasso

278

3.9.67.Ⅱ
4. Picasso

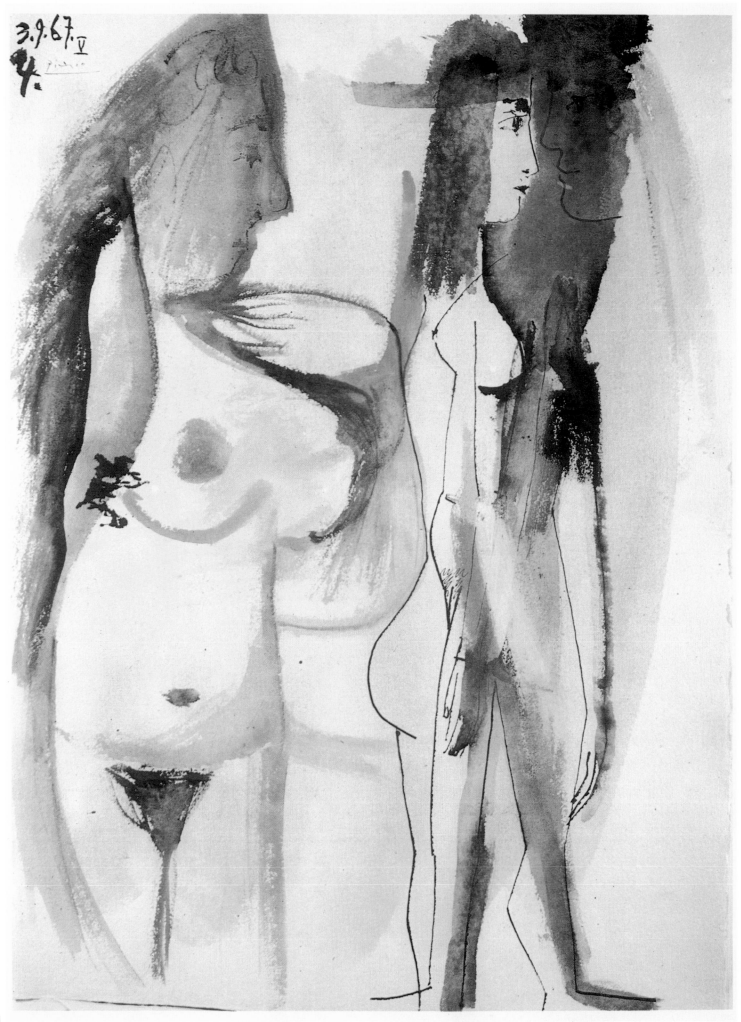

281

282

283

284

18.9.67.

285

289

290

291

292

293

294

295

296

297

298

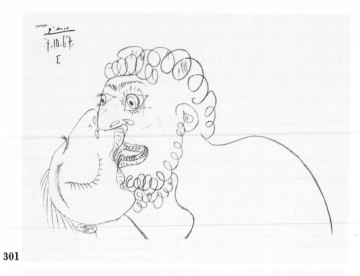

301

302

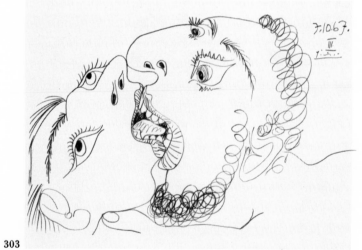

303

304

305

306

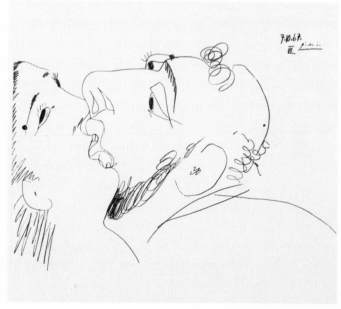

307

308

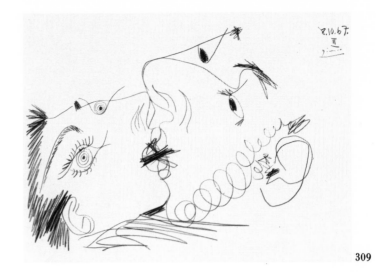

309

310

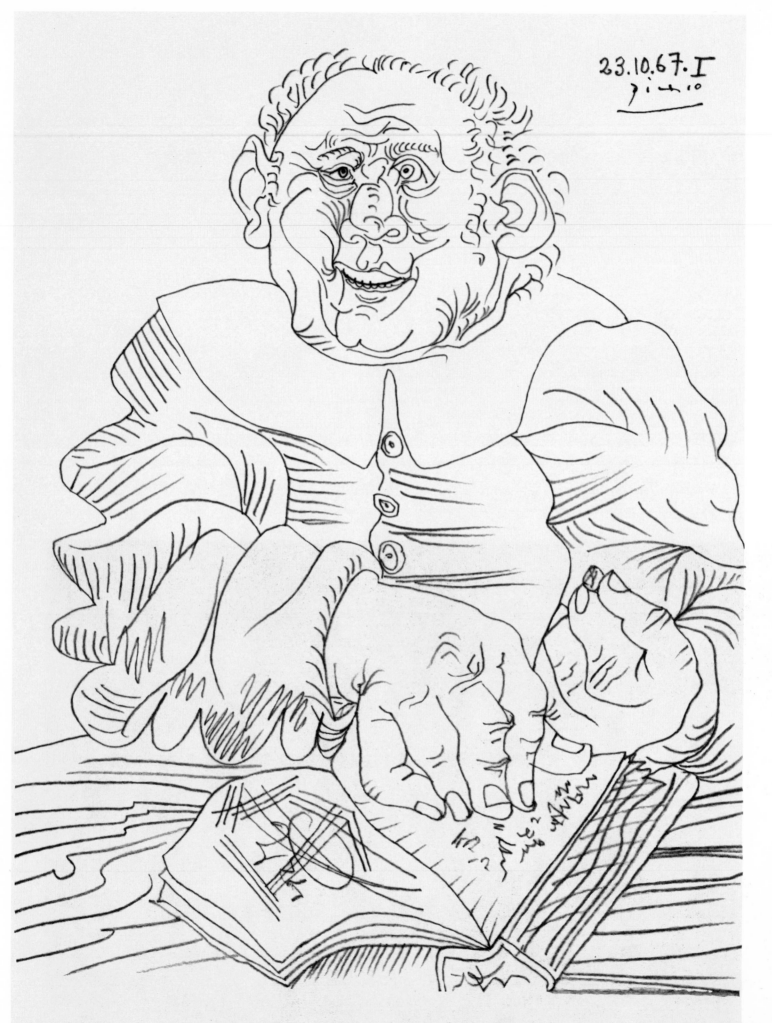

23.10.67. I

311

312

313

315

316

319

320

321

322

323

325

326

30.12.67.

327

328

329

330

331

332

333

334

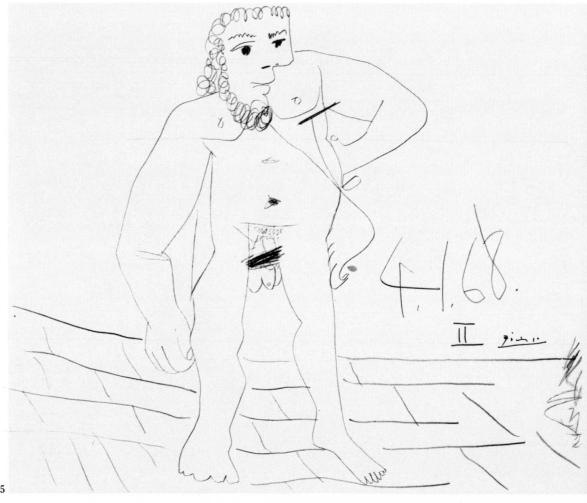

335

336

337

338

341

342

343

344

345

27.1.68. VI   346

27.1.68. V

347

27.1.68.
VII
348

28.1.68. I

28.1.68.II

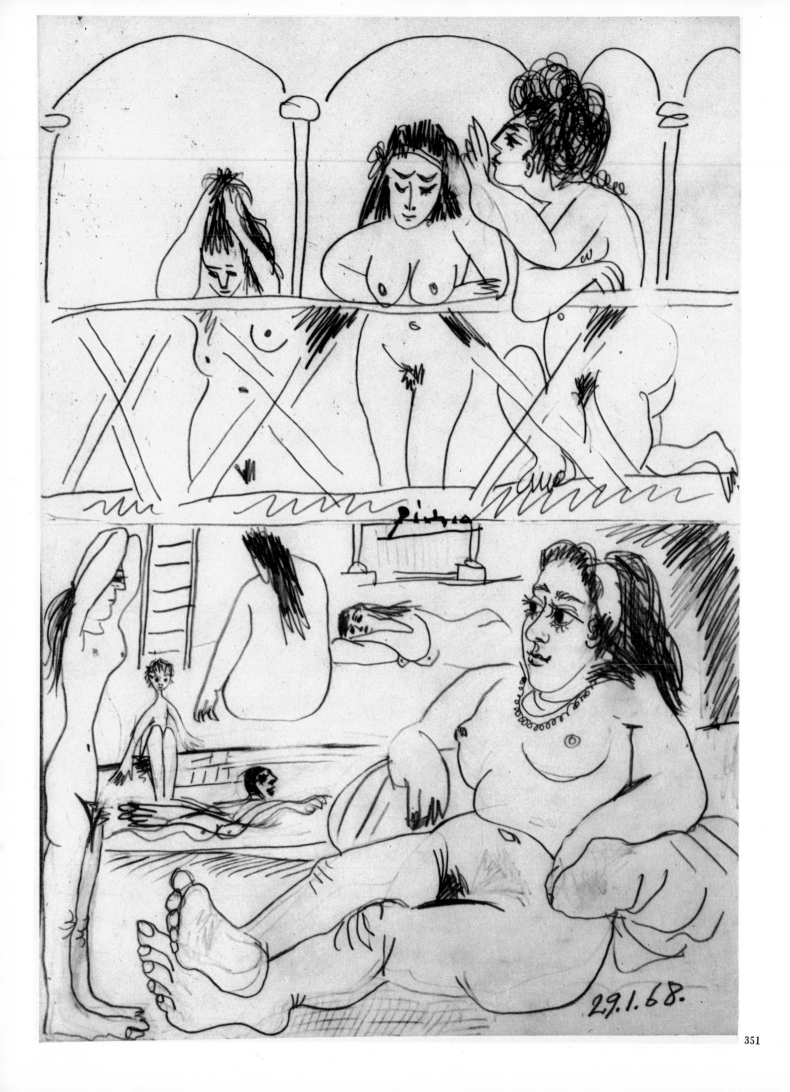

351

352

353

354

355

356

357

358

359

2.68.II

362

363

364

365

366

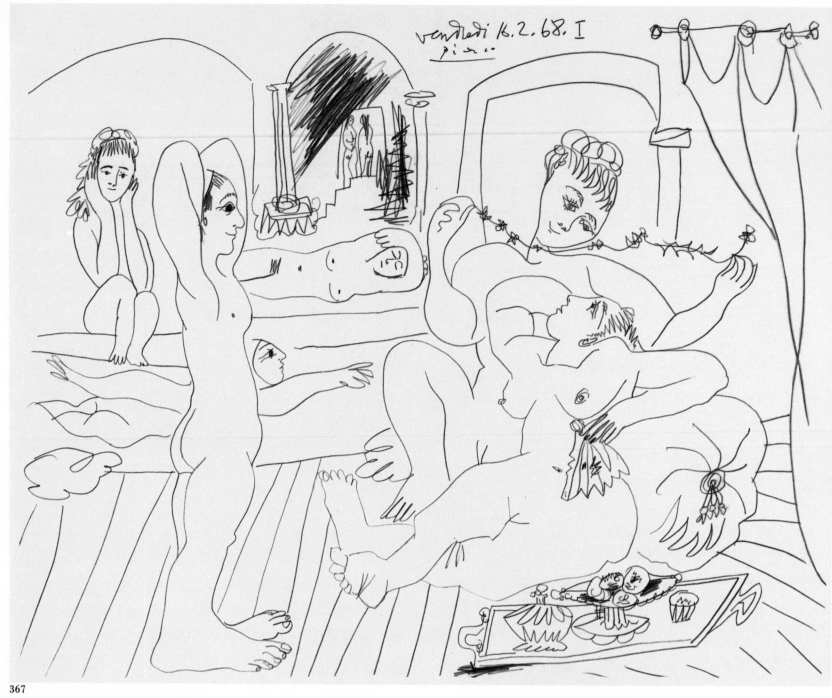

367

368

369

372

375

373

374

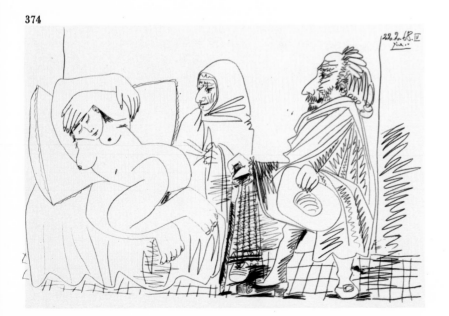

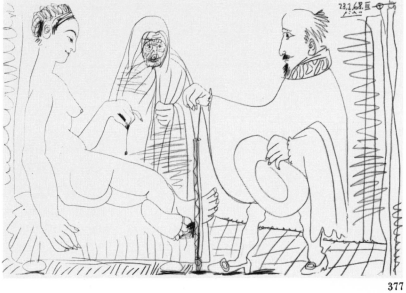

379

381

382

383

384

385

388

389

390

391

392

393

394

395

396

398

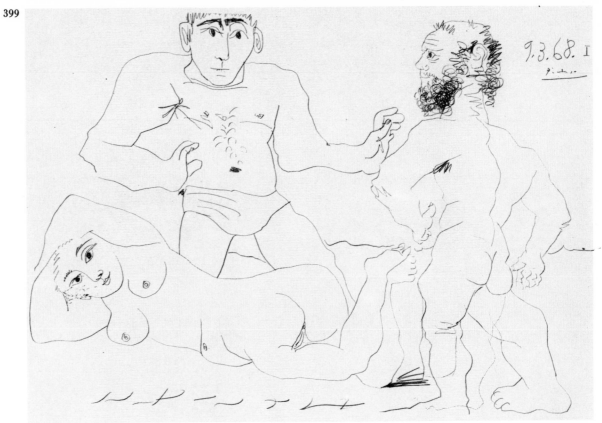

9.3.68. I

401

402

14.3.68. III

404

405

LIST OF PLATES

1. 4–11–66 - VI. Ink, $14\frac{5}{8} \times 21''$.	52. 12–31–66 - II. Pencil, $18\frac{1}{8} \times 21\frac{5}{8}''$.
2. 3–27–66 - Pencil, $10\frac{5}{8} \times 19\frac{3}{4}''$.	53. 12–31–66 - III. Bistre pencil, $18\frac{1}{8} \times 21\frac{5}{8}''$.
3. 4–21–66 - II. Pencil, $24 \times 19\frac{3}{8}''$.	54. 12–31–66 - IV. Bistre pencil, $18\frac{1}{8} \times 21\frac{5}{8}''$.
4. 4–21–66 - I. 7–23–66 - Colored pencil, $24 \times 19\frac{5}{8}''$.	55. 1–1–67 - Bistre pencil, $18\frac{1}{8} \times 21\frac{5}{8}''$.
5. 4–21–66 - III. Wash, $24 \times 19\frac{3}{8}''$.	56. 1–2–67 - I. Bistre pencil, $19\frac{5}{8} \times 24''$.
6. 4–22–66 - Wash and white chalk, $24 \times 19\frac{5}{8}''$.	57. 1–2–67 - II. Bistre pencil, $19\frac{5}{8} \times 24''$.
7. 5–15–66 - I. Bistre pencil, $24 \times 19\frac{5}{8}''$.	58. 1–2–67 - III. Pencil, $19\frac{3}{8} \times 24''$.
8. 5–15–66 - II. Bistre pencil, $24 \times 19\frac{5}{8}''$.	59. 1–2–67 - IV. Bistre pencil, $19\frac{3}{8} \times 24''$.
9. 5–15–66 - III. Bistre pencil, $24 \times 19\frac{3}{8}''$.	60. 1–2–67 - V. Pencil, $19\frac{3}{8} \times 24''$.
10. 5–16–66 - I. Bistre pencil, $24 \times 19\frac{5}{8}''$.	61. 1–2–67 - VI. Pencil, $19\frac{3}{8} \times 24''$.
11. 5–16–66 - II. Pencil, $24 \times 19\frac{3}{8}''$.	62. 1–2–67 - VII. Pencil, $19\frac{3}{8} \times 24''$.
12. 5–16–66 - Pencil, $24 \times 19\frac{3}{8}''$.	63. 1–3–67 - I. Bistre pencil, $19\frac{5}{8} \times 24''$.
13. 5–16–66 - IV. Pencil, $24 \times 19\frac{3}{8}''$.	64. 1–3–67 - II. Bistre pencil, $19\frac{5}{8} \times 24''$.
14. 6–8–66 - I. Colored pencil, $21 \times 14\frac{5}{8}''$.	65. 1–4–67 - Colored pencil, $19\frac{5}{8} \times 24''$.
15. 7–11–66 - II. Colored pencil, $19\frac{5}{8} \times 24''$.	66. 1–5–67 - Colored pencil, $19\frac{5}{8} \times 24''$.
16. 7–22–66 - I. Colored pencil, $19\frac{5}{8} \times 24''$.	67. 1–6–67 - I. Colored pencil, $19\frac{5}{8} \times 24''$.
17. 7–22–66 - II. Colored pencil, $19\frac{3}{8} \times 24''$.	68. 1–6–67 - II. Colored pencil, $19\frac{5}{8} \times 24''$.
18. 11–18–66 - I. Pencil, $13 \times 16\frac{1}{2}''$.	69. 1–7–67 - II. Colored pencil, $19\frac{5}{8} \times 24''$.
19. 11–18–66 - III. Pencil, $13 \times 16\frac{1}{2}''$.	70. 1–7–67 - III. Colored pencil, $19\frac{3}{8} \times 24''$.
20. 11–18–66 - II. Pencil, $13 \times 16\frac{1}{2}''$.	71. 1–7–67 - I. Colored pencil, $19\frac{5}{8} \times 24''$.
21. 11–4/5–66 - Pencil and colored pencil, $24 \times 19\frac{5}{8}''$.	72. 1–9–67 - I. Colored pencil, $19\frac{3}{8} \times 24''$.
22. 11–30–66 - I. Pencil, $13 \times 16\frac{1}{2}''$.	73. 1–9–67 - II. Colored pencil, $19\frac{5}{8} \times 24''$.
23. 11–30–66 - II. Pencil, $13 \times 16\frac{1}{2}''$.	74. 1–9–67 - III. Colored pencil, $19\frac{3}{8} \times 24''$.
24. 12–1–66 - Pencil, $18\frac{1}{8} \times 21\frac{5}{8}''$.	75. 1–9–67 - IV. Colored pencil, $19\frac{5}{8} \times 24''$.
25. 12–11–66 - Bistre pencil, $14\frac{5}{8} \times 21\frac{1}{4}''$.	76. 1–20–67 - I. Pencil, $19\frac{5}{8} \times 25\frac{5}{8}''$.
26. 12–22–66 - Colored pencil, $19\frac{5}{8} \times 24''$.	77. 1–20–67 - II. Bistre pencil, $19\frac{5}{8} \times 25\frac{5}{8}''$.
27. 12–22–66 - II. Bistre pencil, $19\frac{5}{8} \times 24''$.	78. 1–11/12–67 - Colored pencil, $19\frac{5}{8} \times 25\frac{5}{8}''$.
28. 12–23–66 - I. Bistre pencil, $19\frac{5}{8} \times 24''$.	79. 1–20–67 - III. Bistre pencil, $19\frac{5}{8} \times 25\frac{5}{8}''$.
29. 12–23–66 - II. Bistre pencil, $19\frac{5}{8} \times 24''$.	80. 1–20–67 - V. Bistre pencil, $19\frac{5}{8} \times 25\frac{5}{8}''$.
30. 12–23–66 - III. Pencil, $19\frac{3}{8} \times 24''$.	81. 1–20–67 - VII. Pencil, $19\frac{5}{8} \times 25\frac{5}{8}''$.
31. 12–23–66 - IV. 12–24–66 - Bistre pencil, $19\frac{5}{8} \times 24''$.	82. 1–20–67 - IV. Bistre pencil, $19\frac{5}{8} \times 25\frac{5}{8}''$.
32. 12–24–66 - Pencil, $19\frac{3}{8} \times 24''$.	83. 1–20–67 - VI. Bistre pencil, $19\frac{5}{8} \times 25\frac{5}{8}''$.
33. 12–25–66 - I. Colored pencil, $19\frac{3}{8} \times 24''$.	84. 1–20–67 - VIII. Bistre pencil, $19\frac{5}{8} \times 25\frac{5}{8}''$.
34. 12–25–66 - II. Bistre pencil, $19\frac{5}{8} \times 24''$.	85. 1–22–67 - I. Colored pencil, $19\frac{5}{8} \times 25\frac{3}{4}''$.
35. 12–25–66 - III. Pencil, $19\frac{3}{8} \times 24''$.	86. 1–23–67 - I. Colored pencil, $19\frac{5}{8} \times 25\frac{5}{8}''$.
36. 12–26–66 - II. Pencil, $21\frac{5}{8} \times 18\frac{1}{8}''$.	87. 1–26–67 - I. Wash, $20\frac{1}{2} \times 25\frac{1}{2}''$.
37. 12–26–66 - I. Bistre pencil, $21\frac{5}{8} \times 18\frac{1}{8}''$.	88. 1–26–67 - II. Wash, $19\frac{5}{8} \times 25\frac{5}{8}''$.
38. 12–27–66 - I. Bistre pencil, $21\frac{5}{8} \times 18\frac{1}{8}''$.	89. 1–26–67 - III. Wash, $19\frac{5}{8} \times 25\frac{5}{8}''$.
39. 12–27–66 - II. 5–4/5–67 - Colored pencil, $21\frac{5}{8} \times 18\frac{1}{8}''$.	90. 1–26–67 - IV. Wash, $19\frac{5}{8} \times 25\frac{5}{8}''$.
40. 12–27–66 - III. Bistre pencil, $21\frac{5}{8} \times 18\frac{1}{8}''$.	91. 2–3–67 - I. Bistre pencil, $18\frac{7}{8} \times 25''$.
41. 12–27–66 - IV. Pencil, $18\frac{1}{8} \times 21\frac{5}{8}''$.	92. 2–3–67 - II. Bistre pencil, $18\frac{7}{8} \times 25''$.
42. 12–27–66 - V. Bistre pencil, $18\frac{1}{8} \times 21\frac{5}{8}''$.	93. 2–3–67 - III. Bistre pencil, $18\frac{7}{8} \times 25''$.
43. 12–27–66 - VI. Bistre pencil, $21\frac{5}{8} \times 18\frac{1}{8}''$.	94. 2–3–67 - IV. Bistre pencil, $18\frac{7}{8} \times 25''$.
44. 12–27–66 - VII. Bistre pencil, $21\frac{5}{8} \times 18\frac{1}{8}''$.	95. 2–4–67 - I. Colored pencil, $20\frac{1}{2} \times 25\frac{1}{4}''$.
45. 12–29–66 - I. Bistre pencil, $21\frac{5}{8} \times 18\frac{1}{8}''$.	96. 2–4–67 - II. Colored pencil, $19\frac{5}{8} \times 25\frac{5}{8}''$.
46. 12–29–66 - II. Bistre pencil, $21\frac{5}{8} \times 18\frac{1}{8}''$.	97. 2–4–67 - IV. Colored pencil, $19\frac{5}{8} \times 25\frac{5}{8}''$.
47. 12–29–66 - III. Bistre pencil, $21\frac{5}{8} \times 18\frac{1}{8}''$.	98. 2–4–67 - VI. Colored pencil, $19\frac{5}{8} \times 25\frac{5}{8}''$.
48. 12–30–66 - I. Bistre pencil, $21\frac{5}{8} \times 18\frac{1}{8}''$.	99. 2–4–67 - III. Colored pencil, $19\frac{5}{8} \times 25\frac{5}{8}''$.
49. 12–30–66 - II. Bistre pencil, $21\frac{5}{8} \times 18\frac{1}{8}''$.	100. 2–4–67 - V. Colored pencil, $19\frac{5}{8} \times 25\frac{5}{8}''$.
50. 12–30–66 - III. Colored pencil, $21\frac{5}{8} \times 18\frac{1}{8}''$.	101. 2–5–67 - I. Blue pencil, $19\frac{5}{8} \times 25\frac{5}{8}''$.
51. 12–31–66 - I. Pencil, $18\frac{1}{8} \times 21\frac{5}{8}''$.	102. 2–5–67 - II. Colored pencil, $19\frac{5}{8} \times 25\frac{5}{8}''$.

103. 2–5–67 - III. Colored pencil, $20\frac{1}{2}\times25\frac{1}{4}''$.
104. 2–5–67 - VI. Colored pencil, $20\frac{1}{2}\times25\frac{1}{4}''$.
105. 2–5–67 - IV. Colored pencil, $19\frac{5}{8}\times25\frac{5}{8}''$.
106. 2–5–67 - V. Colored pencil, $19\frac{5}{8}\times25\frac{5}{8}''$.
107. 2–9–67 - I. Wash, $20\frac{1}{2}\times25\frac{1}{4}''$.
108. 2–9–67 - III. Wash, $20\frac{1}{2}\times25\frac{1}{4}''$.
109. 2–9–67 - IV. Wash, $19\frac{5}{8}\times25\frac{5}{8}''$.
110. 2–9–67 - V. Wash, $25\frac{5}{8}\times19\frac{5}{8}''$.
111. 2–9–67 - VI. Wash, $25\frac{5}{8}\times19\frac{5}{8}''$.
112. 2–10–67 - I. Wash, $25\frac{5}{8}\times19\frac{5}{8}''$.
113. 2–10–67 - II. Wash, $25\frac{5}{8}\times19\frac{5}{8}''$.
114. 2–10–67 - III. Wash, $25\frac{5}{8}\times19\frac{5}{8}''$.
115. 2–10–67 - IV. Wash, $25\frac{5}{8}\times19\frac{5}{8}''$.
116. 2–11–67 - I. Wash, $25\frac{5}{8}\times19\frac{5}{8}''$.
117. 2–11–67 - II. Wash, $25\frac{5}{8}\times19\frac{5}{8}''$.
118. 2–11–67 - III. Wash, $25\frac{5}{8}\times19\frac{5}{8}''$.
119. 2–12–67 - Wash, colored pencil, $25\frac{5}{8}\times19\frac{5}{8}''$.
120. 2–13–67 - Wash, $20\frac{7}{8}\times24\frac{3}{4}''$.
121. 2–15–67 - V. Wash, $12\frac{1}{2}\times18\frac{7}{8}''$.
122. 2–22–67 - I. Colored pencil, $19\frac{3}{8}\times24\frac{3}{8}''$.
123. 2–26–67 - I. 8–22–67 - India ink, colored pencil, $18\frac{1}{4}\times24\frac{1}{4}''$.
124. 2–26–67 - II. Colored pencil, $24\frac{1}{4}\times18\frac{1}{4}''$.
125. 2–26–67 - III. Blue pencil, $25\frac{5}{8}\times19\frac{5}{8}''$.
126. 2–26–67 - IV. Colored pencil, $25\frac{5}{8}\times19\frac{3}{8}''$.
127. 2–26–67 - V. Colored pencil, $25\frac{5}{8}\times19\frac{3}{8}''$.
128. 2–26–67 - VI. Wash, colored pencil, $25\frac{5}{8}\times19\frac{3}{8}''$.
129. 3–1–67 - I. Blue pencil, $29\frac{7}{8}\times19\frac{1}{4}''$.
130. 3–1–67 - II. Wash, $24\frac{3}{4}\times18\frac{1}{2}''$.
131. 3–1–67 - III. Wash, $24\frac{3}{4}\times18\frac{1}{2}''$.
132. 3–1–67 - IV. Wash, $24\frac{3}{4}\times18\frac{1}{2}''$.
133. 3–4/5–67 - Colored pencil, $19\frac{1}{2}\times25\frac{5}{8}''$.
134. 3–5–67 - I. Colored pencil, $19\times25\frac{5}{8}''$.
135. 3–5–67 - II. Colored pencil, $19\frac{1}{2}\times25\frac{5}{8}''$.
136. 3–6–67 - I. Colored pencil, $19\frac{1}{4}\times25\frac{5}{8}''$.
137. 3–6–67 - II. Colored pencil, $19\frac{1}{2}\times25\frac{5}{8}''$.
138. 3–6–67 - III. Colored pencil, $19\frac{1}{2}\times25\frac{5}{8}''$.
139. 3–6–67 - IV. Pencil, $19\frac{1}{2}\times25\frac{5}{8}''$.
140. 3–7–67 - I. Wash, $19\frac{1}{2}\times25\frac{5}{8}''$.
141. 3–7–67 - II. Wash, $19\frac{1}{2}\times25\frac{5}{8}''$.
142. 3–7–67 - IV. India ink, wash, $19\frac{1}{2}\times25\frac{5}{8}''$.
143. 3–7–67 - III. Wash, $19\frac{1}{2}\times25\frac{5}{8}''$.
144. 3–8–67 - I. Wash, $19\frac{1}{2}\times25\frac{5}{8}''$.
145. 3–8–67 - III. Wash, $19\frac{1}{2}\times25\frac{5}{8}''$.
146. 3–8–67 - II. Wash, $19\frac{1}{2}\times25\frac{5}{8}''$.
147. 3–9–67 - II. Wash, $19\frac{1}{2}\times25\frac{5}{8}''$.
148. 3–9–67 - I. 3–14/15–67 - Wash, $19\frac{1}{2}\times25\frac{5}{8}''$.
149. 3–9–67 - III. Wash, $19\frac{1}{2}\times25\frac{5}{8}''$.
150. 3–10–67 - II. Wash, $19\frac{1}{4}\times29\frac{3}{4}''$.
151. 3–10–67 - I. Wash, $19\frac{1}{2}\times29\frac{3}{4}''$.
152. 3–12–67 - Wash, $19\frac{1}{4}\times29\frac{3}{4}''$.
153. 3–10–67 - IV. Wash, $18\frac{1}{2}\times24\frac{3}{4}''$.

154. 3–11–67 - Wash, $19\frac{3}{8}\times29\frac{1}{2}''$.
155. 3–10–67 - III. 3–13–67 - Wash, $19\frac{3}{8}\times29\frac{1}{2}''$.
156. 3–10–67 - III. 3–13–67 - Wash, $19\frac{3}{8}\times59''$. *Drawings 154 and 155 combined.*
157. 3–15–67 - I. Wash, $15\frac{1}{4}\times19\frac{3}{8}''$.
158. 3–15–67 - II. Wash, $19\frac{5}{8}\times15\frac{1}{4}''$.
159. 3–15–67 - III. 4–14–67 - Wash, $15\frac{1}{4}\times19\frac{3}{8}''$.
160. 3–15–67 - IV. 3–18–67 - Wash, $19\frac{5}{8}\times23\frac{3}{8}''$.
161. 3–18–67 - Pencil, $23\frac{5}{8}\times19\frac{5}{8}''$.
162. 3–21–67 - Wash, $15\times19\frac{5}{8}''$.
163. 5–29–67 - Wash and chalk, $19\frac{5}{8}\times24''$.
164. 5–29–67 - Wash, $19\frac{5}{8}\times24''$.
165. 5–29–67 - Wash, $19\frac{5}{8}\times24''$.
166. 6–2–67 - India ink, $19\frac{3}{8}\times23\frac{3}{4}''$.
167. 6–3–67 - India ink, $19\frac{3}{8}\times23\frac{3}{4}''$.
168. 6–5–67 - I. India ink, $19\frac{3}{8}\times23\frac{3}{4}''$.
169. 6–5–67 - III. India ink, $23\frac{3}{4}\times19\frac{3}{8}$ *(verso of drawing n° 168)*.
170. 6–5–67 - IV. India ink, $19\frac{3}{8}\times23\frac{3}{4}''$.
171. 6–5–67 - II. 6–8–67 - India ink, $23\frac{3}{4}\times19\frac{3}{8}''$.
172. 6–6–67 - I. India ink, $19\frac{3}{8}\times23\frac{3}{4}''$.
173. 6–6–67 - III. India ink, $19\frac{3}{8}\times23\frac{3}{4}''$.
174. 6–6–67 - IV. India ink, $19\frac{3}{8}\times23\frac{3}{4}''$ *(verso of drawing n° 167)*.
175. 6–6–67 - V. India ink, $19\frac{3}{8}\times23\frac{3}{4}''$.
176. 6–5–67 - 6–7–67 - India ink, $19\frac{3}{8}\times23\frac{3}{4}''$.
177. 6–17–67 - VI. Charcoal, $25\times19\frac{3}{8}''$.
178. 6–17–67 - II. Oil and charcoal, $18\frac{3}{4}\times24\frac{1}{4}''$.
179. 6–17–67 - III. Oil and charcoal, $24\frac{1}{2}\times18\frac{7}{8}''$.
180. 6–17–67 - IV. Oil, colored pencil, and charcoal, $24\frac{3}{8}\times18\frac{1}{4}''$.
181. 6–17–67 - V. Oil, colored pencil, $25\times19\frac{1}{8}''$.
182. 6–28–67 - Pencil, $12\frac{3}{4}\times19\frac{5}{8}''$.
183. 6–28–67 - Pencil, $12\frac{3}{4}\times9\frac{3}{4}''$ *(verso of drawing n° 185)*.
184. 6–28–67 - II. Pencil, $12\frac{3}{4}\times10''$.
185. 6–28–67 - IV. Bistre pencil, $9\frac{3}{4}\times12\frac{3}{4}''$.
186. 6–28–67 - V. Bistre pencil, $12\frac{7}{8}\times19\frac{5}{8}''$.
187. 6–28–67 - III. Bistre pencil, $12\frac{7}{8}\times10''$ *(verso of drawing n° 184)*.
188. 6–28–67 - Colored pencil, $19\frac{5}{8}\times12\frac{3}{4}''$ *(verso of drawing n° 182)*.
189. 6–28–67 - VI. Bistre pencil, $13\times19\frac{5}{8}''$.
190. 7–1–67 - Pencil, $14\frac{3}{4}\times20\frac{1}{4}''$.
191. 7–1–67 - II. Pencil, bistre pencil, $8\times14\frac{3}{4}''$.
192. 7–1–67 - III. Bistre pencil, $14\frac{3}{4}\times8''$ *(verso of drawing n° 191)*.
193. 7–1–67 - IV. Pencil, $14\frac{7}{8}\times12\frac{3}{4}''$.
194. 7–1–67 - V. Pencil, $10\frac{1}{2}\times14\frac{3}{4}''$.
195. 7–1–67 - VI. Pencil, $10\frac{3}{8}\times14\frac{3}{4}''$.
196. 7–1–67 - VII. Pencil, $10\frac{1}{2}\times14\frac{3}{4}''$.
197. 7–1–67 - VIII. Bistre pencil, $10\frac{1}{2}\times14\frac{7}{8}''$.
198. 7–1–67 - IX. Pencil, $14\frac{7}{8}\times20\frac{1}{4}''$.
199. 7–1–67 - X. Pencil, $14\frac{7}{8}\times16\frac{5}{8}''$.
200. 7–2–67 - II. India ink, $14\frac{3}{4}\times20\frac{3}{4}''$.
201. 7–2–67 - I. India ink, $14\frac{3}{4}\times20\frac{5}{8}''$.
202. 7–2–67 - III. India ink, $14\frac{3}{4}\times20\frac{5}{8}''$.

252

203. 7–2–67 - IV. India ink, $14\frac{3}{4} \times 20\frac{5}{8}''$.
204. 7–3–67 - I. India ink, $14\frac{7}{8} \times 20\frac{5}{8}''$.
205. 7–3–67 - II. India ink, $14\frac{3}{4} \times 20\frac{5}{8}''$.
206. 7–4–67 - I. India ink, $14\frac{3}{4} \times 20\frac{5}{8}''$.
207. 7–4–67 - II. India ink, $14\frac{5}{8} \times 20\frac{5}{8}''$ (verso of drawing nº 208).
208. 7–4–67 - III. India ink, $14\frac{5}{8} \times 20\frac{5}{8}''$.
209. 7–5–67 - India ink, colored pencil, $14\frac{5}{8} \times 20\frac{5}{8}''$.
210. 7–5–67 - II. India ink, colored pencil, $14\frac{5}{8} \times 20\frac{5}{8}''$.
211. 7–5–67 - III. India ink, $14\frac{5}{8} \times 20\frac{5}{8}''$.
212. 7–7–67 - II. India ink, $19\frac{1}{2} \times 23\frac{3}{4}''$.
213. 7–10–67 - I. India ink, $20\frac{5}{8} \times 29\frac{1}{4}''$.
214. 7–5–67 - IV. India ink, $14\frac{7}{8} \times 20\frac{5}{8}''$.
215. 7–10–67 - II. India ink, $20\frac{5}{8} \times 29\frac{1}{4}''$.
216. 7–10–67 - III. India ink, $19\frac{3}{4} \times 25\frac{1}{4}''$.
217. 7–11–67 - India ink, $19\frac{3}{4} \times 25\frac{1}{4}''$.
218. 7–12–67 - I. India ink, $19\frac{3}{4} \times 25\frac{1}{4}''$.
219. 7–12–67 - II. India ink, $19\frac{3}{4} \times 25\frac{1}{4}''$.
220. 7–12–67 - III. India ink, $19\frac{3}{4} \times 25\frac{1}{2}''$.
221. 7–13–67 - India ink, gouache, $22\frac{1}{4} \times 29\frac{1}{2}''$.
222. 7–7–67 - India ink, gouache, and watercolor, $19\frac{1}{2} \times 24\frac{1}{4}''$.
223. 7–17–67 - I. India ink, $11\frac{1}{8} \times 18\frac{1}{8}''$.
224. 7–17–67 - II. India Ink, $11\frac{1}{4} \times 18\frac{1}{4}''$.
225. 7–17–67 - III. India ink, $22\frac{1}{4} \times 29\frac{1}{2}''$.
226. 7–18–67 - I and III. Colored pencil, $29\frac{1}{2} \times 22\frac{1}{4}''$.
227. 7–18–67 - II. Colored pencil, $29\frac{1}{2} \times 22\frac{1}{4}''$.
228. 7–20–67 - India ink, $14\frac{7}{8} \times 11''$.
229. 7–20–67 - IV. India ink, $14\frac{7}{8} \times 7\frac{5}{8}''$.
230. 7–20–67 - VII. India ink, $14\frac{7}{8} \times 7\frac{5}{8}''$ (verso of drawing nº 229).
231. 7–20–67 - VI. India ink, $14\frac{5}{8} \times 14\frac{3}{4}''$.
232. 7–20–67 - II. India ink, $14\frac{5}{8} \times 14\frac{3}{4}''$ (verso of drawing nº 231).
233. 7–19–67 - India ink, colored pencil, $22\frac{1}{4} \times 19\frac{1}{2}''$.
234. 7–22–67 - Colored pencil, $22\frac{1}{4} \times 19\frac{1}{2}''$.
235. 7–20–67 - Colored pencil, $14\frac{3}{4} \times 11\frac{1}{2}''$.
236. 7–20–67 - Colored pencil, $14\frac{3}{4} \times 11''$.
237. 7–23–67 - India ink, $19\frac{1}{2} \times 22\frac{1}{4}''$.
238. 7–23–67 - II. India ink, $19\frac{1}{2} \times 22\frac{1}{4}''$.
239. 7–23–67 - IV. India ink, colored pencil, $19\frac{1}{2} \times 22\frac{1}{4}''$.
240. 7–23–67 - V. India ink, $19\frac{1}{2} \times 22\frac{1}{4}''$.
241. 7–24–67 - III. 8–27–67 - India ink, gouache, $19\frac{1}{2} \times 22\frac{1}{4}''$.
242. 7–24–67 - India ink, $19\frac{1}{2} \times 22\frac{1}{4}''$.
243. 7–24–67 - II. India ink, gouache, $19\frac{1}{2} \times 22\frac{1}{4}''$.
244. 7–27–67 - India ink, gouache, $22\frac{1}{4} \times 19\frac{1}{2}''$.
245. 7–30–67 - 8–1–67 - India ink, gouache, $29\frac{1}{2} \times 22\frac{1}{4}''$.
246. 8–1–67 - India ink, gouache, $29\frac{1}{2} \times 22\frac{1}{4}''$.
247. 8–3–67 - India ink, gouache, $29\frac{1}{2} \times 22\frac{1}{4}''$.
248. 7–30–67 - II. India ink, gouache, $29\frac{1}{2} \times 22\frac{1}{4}''$.
249. 8–1–67 - II. India ink, gouache, $29\frac{1}{2} \times 22\frac{1}{4}''$.
250. 8–3–67 - II. India ink, $29\frac{1}{2} \times 22\frac{1}{4}''$.
251. 7–31–67 - India ink, gouache, $29\frac{1}{2} \times 22\frac{1}{4}''$.
252. 8–2–67 - India ink, $29\frac{1}{2} \times 22\frac{1}{4}''$.
253. 8–5–67 - India ink, gouache, $29\frac{1}{2} \times 22\frac{1}{4}''$.

254. 8–7–67 - II. 8–20–67 - India ink, gouache, $22\frac{1}{4} \times 29\frac{1}{2}''$.
255. 8–7–67 - India ink, $29\frac{1}{2} \times 22\frac{1}{4}''$.
256. 8–8–67 - India ink, gouache, $29\frac{1}{2} \times 22\frac{1}{4}''$.
257. 8–18–67 - India ink, $22\frac{1}{4} \times 29\frac{1}{2}''$.
258. 8–19–67 - India ink, $22\frac{1}{4} \times 29\frac{1}{2}''$.
259. 8–18–67 - II. Ink, colored pencil, and gouache, $22\frac{1}{4} \times 29\frac{1}{2}''$.
260. 8–22–67 - India ink, colored pencil, $22\frac{1}{4} \times 29\frac{1}{2}''$.
261. 8–23–67 - Ink, $12\frac{1}{8} \times 8\frac{3}{4}''$.
262. 8–25–67 - India ink, $22\frac{1}{4} \times 29\frac{1}{2}''$.
263. 8–24–67 - India ink, $22\frac{1}{4} \times 29\frac{1}{2}''$.
264. 8–27–67 - India ink, $22\frac{1}{4} \times 29\frac{1}{2}''$.
265. 8–30–67 - Pencil, $22\frac{1}{4} \times 29\frac{1}{2}''$.
266. 8–30–67 - II. Pencil, $22\frac{1}{4} \times 29\frac{1}{2}''$.
267. 8–30–67 - Pencil, $22\frac{1}{4} \times 29\frac{1}{2}''$.
268. 8–31–67 - II. Pencil, $22\frac{1}{4} \times 29\frac{1}{2}''$.
269. 8–31–67 - I. Pencil, $22\frac{1}{4} \times 29\frac{1}{2}''$.
270. 8–31–67 - III. Pencil, $22\frac{1}{4} \times 29\frac{1}{2}''$.
271. 9–1–67 - I. Pencil, $22\frac{1}{4} \times 29\frac{1}{2}''$.
272. 9–1–67 - II. India ink, $22\frac{1}{4} \times 29\frac{1}{2}''$.
273. 9–1–67 - III. Colored pencil, $22\frac{1}{4} \times 29\frac{1}{2}''$.
274. 9–1–67 - IV. Blue pencil, $22\frac{1}{4} \times 29\frac{1}{2}''$.
275. 9–1–67 - V. Colored pencil, $22\frac{1}{4} \times 29\frac{1}{2}''$.
276. 9–2–67 - I. Pencil, $29\frac{1}{2} \times 22\frac{1}{4}''$.
277. 9–2–67 - II. Pencil, $29\frac{1}{2} \times 22\frac{1}{4}''$.
278. 9–3–67 - I. Pencil, gouache, $29\frac{1}{2} \times 22\frac{1}{4}''$.
279. 9–3–67 - II. 9–4–67 - Pencil, gouache, $29\frac{1}{2} \times 22\frac{1}{4}''$.
280. 9–3–67 - III. Pencil, gouache, $29\frac{1}{2} \times 22\frac{1}{4}''$.
281. 9–3–67 - V. 9–4–67 - India ink, gouache, $29\frac{1}{2} \times 22\frac{1}{4}''$.
282. 9–3–67 - IV. Pencil, gouache, $22 \times 29\frac{1}{2}''$.
283. 9–4–67 - Colored pencil, gouache, $22\frac{1}{4} \times 29\frac{1}{2}''$.
284. 9–4–67 - II. Colored pencil, $22\frac{1}{4} \times 29\frac{1}{2}''$.
285. 9–18–67 - III. Pencil, $29\frac{7}{8} \times 22''$.
286. 9–19–67 - Pencil, $22 \times 29\frac{7}{8}''$.
287. 9–19–67 - II. Pencil, $22 \times 29\frac{7}{8}''$.
288. 9–19–67 - III. Pencil, $22 \times 29\frac{7}{8}''$.
289. 9–20–67 - Pencil, $22 \times 29\frac{7}{8}''$.
290. 9–21–67 - Pencil, $22 \times 29\frac{7}{8}''$.
291. 9–25–67 - I. India ink, wash, $22 \times 29\frac{7}{8}''$.
292. 9–25–67 - II. India ink, wash, $22 \times 29\frac{7}{8}''$.
293. 9–6–67 - Colored pencil, $22\frac{1}{4} \times 29\frac{1}{2}''$.
294. 9–29–67 - I. Pencil, $22\frac{1}{4} \times 30''$.
295. 9–29–67 - II. Pencil, $22\frac{1}{4} \times 29\frac{7}{8}''$.
296. 10–1–67 - Pencil, $22\frac{1}{4} \times 29\frac{7}{8}''$.
297. 10–2–67 - Colored pencil, $22 \times 29\frac{7}{8}''$.
298. 10–5–67 - 10–7–67 - II. Pencil and colored pencil, $13 \times 19\frac{7}{8}''$.
299. 10–4–67 - I. Pencil, $12\frac{3}{4} \times 19\frac{5}{8}''$.
300. 10–4–67 - II. Pencil, $12\frac{7}{8} \times 21''$.
301. 10–7–67 - I. Pencil, $13 \times 19\frac{7}{8}''$.
302. 10–7–67 - II. Pencil, $13 \times 19\frac{7}{8}''$.
303. 10–7–67 - III. Pencil, $12\frac{3}{4} \times 19\frac{7}{8}''$.

304.   10–7–67 - IV. Pencil, $19\frac{7}{8} \times 25\frac{3}{4}''$.

305.   10–7–67 - V. Pencil, $19\frac{7}{8} \times 25\frac{3}{4}''$.

306.   10–7–67 - VI. Pencil, $19\frac{7}{8} \times 25\frac{3}{4}''$.

307.   10–7–67 - VII. Pencil, $19\frac{7}{8} \times 25\frac{3}{4}''$.

308.   10–8–67 - I. Pencil, $12\frac{3}{4} \times 19\frac{7}{8}''$.

309.   10–8–67 - II. Pencil, $13 \times 19\frac{7}{8}''$.

310.   10–14–67 - 10–18–67 - Pencil and colored pencil, $11\frac{1}{4} \times 18\frac{1}{4}''$.

311.   10–23–67 - I. Pencil, $11\frac{1}{2} \times 9''$.

312.   10–23–67 - II. Pencil, $8\frac{1}{8} \times 11\frac{1}{2}''$.

313.   10–23–67 - III. Pencil, $9\frac{7}{8} \times 12\frac{7}{8}''$.

314.   10–24–67 - 11–4–67 - Pencil, $12\frac{7}{8} \times 9\frac{7}{8}''$.

315.   11–6–67 - Pencil, $9\frac{7}{8} \times 12\frac{7}{8}''$.

316.   11–7–67 - Pencil, $10 \times 12\frac{7}{8}''$.

317.   11–8–67 - 11–14–67 and 12–25–67 - India ink and gouache, $25\frac{5}{8} \times 22\frac{7}{8}''$.

318.   11–14–67 - India ink, wash, $25\frac{5}{8} \times 19\frac{7}{8}''$.

319.   11–16–67 - Ink, $10\frac{3}{4} \times 8\frac{1}{2}''$.

320.   11–15–67 - Pencil, $9\frac{1}{4} \times 12\frac{5}{8}''$.

321.   11–15–67 - Colored pencil, $12\frac{5}{8} \times 9\frac{1}{4}''$.

322.   11–21–67 - India ink, wash, $19\frac{7}{8} \times 25\frac{5}{8}''$.

323.   12–24–67 - India ink, wash, $19\frac{7}{8} \times 25\frac{3}{4}''$.

324.   12–27–67 - Colored pencil, $17\frac{1}{2} \times 13\frac{3}{4}''$.

325.   12–28–67 - II. India ink, wash, $8\frac{1}{4} \times 10\frac{1}{4}''$.

326.   12–28–67 - III. India ink, wash, $8\frac{1}{4} \times 10\frac{1}{4}''$.

327.   12–30–67 - India ink, wash, $19\frac{7}{8} \times 25\frac{5}{8}''$.

328.   12–31–67 - II. Pencil, $22\frac{1}{4} \times 29\frac{7}{8}''$.

329.   12–31–67 - III. Pencil, $22\frac{1}{4} \times 29\frac{7}{8}''$.

330.   1–1–68 - I. Pencil, $22\frac{1}{4} \times 29\frac{7}{8}''$.

331.   1–1–68 - II. Pencil, $22\frac{1}{8} \times 29\frac{7}{8}''$.

332.   1–1–68 - III. Pencil, $22 \times 29\frac{7}{8}''$.

333.   1–1–68 - IV. Pencil, $19\frac{1}{2} \times 25\frac{5}{8}''$.

334.   1–3–68 - Pencil, $19\frac{1}{2} \times 25\frac{5}{8}''$.

335.   1–4–68 - II. Pencil, $18\frac{7}{8} \times 23\frac{1}{4}''$.

336.   1–4–68 - III. Pencil, $18\frac{7}{8} \times 23\frac{1}{4}''$ (verso of drawing nº 335).

337.   1–4–68 - IV. Pencil, $18\frac{7}{8} \times 23\frac{1}{4}''$.

338.   1–4–68 - V. 3–2–68 - Sanguine and colored pencil, $18\frac{7}{8} \times 23\frac{1}{4}''$.

339.   1–5–68 - II. Pencil, $18\frac{7}{8} \times 23\frac{1}{4}''$.

340.   1–10–68 - I. Pencil, $18\frac{7}{8} \times 23\frac{1}{4}''$.

341.   1–10–68 - II. India ink, wash, $18\frac{7}{8} \times 23\frac{1}{4}''$.

342.   1–27–68 - Pencil, $18\frac{1}{2} \times 22\frac{1}{4}''$.

343.   1–27–68 - II. Pencil, $18\frac{7}{8} \times 23\frac{1}{4}''$.

344.   1–27–68 - III. Pencil, $11\frac{1}{2} \times 18\frac{7}{8}''$.

345.   1–27–68 - IV. Pencil, $11\frac{1}{2} \times 18\frac{7}{8}''$.

346.   1–27–68 - VI. Pencil, $9\frac{1}{2} \times 11\frac{1}{2}''$.

347.   1–27–68 - V. Pencil $11\frac{1}{2} \times 18\frac{7}{8}''$.

348.   1–27–68 - VII. Pencil, $9\frac{3}{8} \times 11\frac{1}{2}''$.

349.   1–28–68 - I. Pencil, $18\frac{7}{8} \times 23''$.

350.   1–28–68 - II. Pencil, $18\frac{7}{8} \times 23\frac{1}{4}''$.

351.   1–29–68 - Pencil, $16\frac{1}{2} \times 11\frac{5}{8}''$.

352.   1–30–68 - II. Pencil, $18\frac{7}{8} \times 23\frac{1}{8}''$.

353.   1–30–68 - I. Pencil, $23 \times 30\frac{1}{4}''$.

354.   1–30–68 - V. Pencil, $11\frac{5}{8} \times 18\frac{7}{8}''$.

355.   1–30–68 - IV. Pencil, $18\frac{7}{8} \times 23\frac{1}{4}''$.

356.   1–30–68 - III. Pencil, $18\frac{7}{8} \times 23\frac{1}{4}''$.

357.   1–30–68 - VI. Pencil, $11\frac{1}{2} \times 18\frac{7}{8}''$.

358.   1–31–68 - Ink, $9\frac{1}{2} \times 12\frac{1}{4}''$.

359.   1–31–68 - Ink, $9\frac{1}{2} \times 12\frac{1}{4}''$ (verso of drawing nº 358).

360.   2–1–68 - Ink, $9\frac{1}{2} \times 12\frac{1}{4}''$.

361.   2–1–68 - Ink, $9\frac{1}{2} \times 12\frac{1}{4}''$ (verso of drawing nº 360).

362.   2–2–68 - I. Ink, $5\frac{1}{8} \times 3\frac{3}{8}''$.

363.   2–2–68 - II. Ink, $5\frac{1}{8} \times 3\frac{3}{8}''$.

364.   2–3–68 - Ink, $9\frac{1}{4} \times 12\frac{5}{8}''$.

365.   2–16–68 - V. India ink, $18\frac{1}{2} \times 25''$.

366.   2–16–68 - VI. Ink, $18\frac{1}{2} \times 25''$.

367.   2–16–68 - I. Pencil, $19\frac{1}{4} \times 23\frac{5}{8}''$.

368.   2–16–68 - II. Pencil, $19 \times 23\frac{5}{8}''$.

369.   2–16–68 - III. Pencil, $18\frac{7}{8} \times 23\frac{1}{4}''$.

370.   2–16–68 - VII. Pencil, $19\frac{1}{4} \times 29\frac{3}{4}''$.

371.   2–16–68 - IV. Pencil, $18\frac{7}{8} \times 23\frac{1}{4}''$.

372.   2–22–68 - I. Pencil, $19\frac{1}{2} \times 29\frac{3}{4}''$.

373.   2–22–68 - III. Pencil, $19\frac{1}{4} \times 29\frac{3}{4}''$.

374.   2–22–68 - IV. Pencil, $19\frac{3}{8} \times 28\frac{7}{8}''$.

375.   2–23–68 - I. Pencil, $19\frac{3}{8} \times 29\frac{7}{8}''$.

376.   2–23–68 - II. Pencil, $19\frac{3}{8} \times 29\frac{3}{4}''$.

377.   2–23–68 - III. Pencil, $19\frac{3}{8} \times 29\frac{3}{4}''$.

378.   2–22–68 - II. Pencil, $19\frac{3}{8} \times 29\frac{7}{8}''$.

379.   2–24–68 - Pencil, $19\frac{3}{8} \times 29\frac{3}{4}''$.

380.   2–26–68 - I. Pencil, $18\frac{1}{2} \times 25''$.

381.   2–26–68 - II. Pencil and sanguine, $18\frac{1}{2} \times 25''$.

382.   2–26–68 - III. Pencil, sanguine, and chalk, $18\frac{1}{2} \times 24\frac{7}{8}''$.

383.   2–26–68 - IV. Pencil and sanguine, $18\frac{5}{8} \times 25''$.

384.   2–27–68 - Pencil and sanguine, $18\frac{1}{2} \times 24\frac{7}{8}''$.

385.   2–28–68 - I. Pencil, $19\frac{3}{8} \times 29\frac{7}{8}''$.

386.   2–28–68 - II. Pencil, $19\frac{1}{4} \times 25\frac{5}{8}''$.

387.   2–28–68 - III. 3–19–68 - Pencil, sanguine, and chalk, $19\frac{1}{4} \times 25\frac{7}{8}''$.

388.   2–29–68 - II. Pencil and colored pencil, $19\frac{3}{8} \times 29\frac{7}{8}''$.

389.   2–29–68 - I. Pencil, $19\frac{3}{8} \times 29\frac{7}{8}''$.

390.   2–29–68 - IV. Pencil, $19\frac{3}{8} \times 29\frac{7}{8}''$.

391.   2–29–68 - III. Pencil, $19\frac{3}{8} \times 29\frac{7}{8}''$.

392.   3–4/5/6–68 - Colored pencil, $18\frac{7}{8} \times 23\frac{1}{4}''$.

393.   3–1–68 - Sanguine, colored pencil, and pencil, $19\frac{3}{8} \times 29\frac{5}{8}''$.

394.   3–5–68 - Pencil, $18\frac{7}{8} \times 23\frac{1}{4}''$.

395.   3–7–68 - Pencil, $19\frac{3}{8} \times 29\frac{3}{4}''$.

396.   3–8–68 - I. Pencil, $19\frac{3}{8} \times 29\frac{7}{8}''$.

397.   3–8–68 - II. Pencil, $19\frac{1}{4} \times 29\frac{7}{8}''$.

398.   3–8–68 - IV. Pencil. $19\frac{1}{4} \times 29\frac{5}{8}''$.

399.   3–9–68 - I. Pencil, $19\frac{3}{8} \times 29\frac{3}{4}''$.

400.   3–9–68 - IV. Pencil, $19\frac{1}{4} \times 29\frac{5}{8}''$.

401.   3–14–68 - I. Pencil, $19\frac{3}{8} \times 29\frac{7}{8}''$.

402.   3–14–68 - II. Pencil, $19\frac{3}{8} \times 29\frac{7}{8}''$.

403.   3–14–68 - III. Pencil, $19\frac{3}{8} \times 29\frac{7}{8}''$.

404.   3–14–68 - IV. Pencil, $18\frac{1}{2} \times 25''$.

405.   3–15–68 - Pencil, $18\frac{1}{2} \times 25''$.